THE COUNTRY PARSON

THE
COUNTRY PARSON

Simon Goodenough

DAVID & CHARLES
Newton Abbot   London   North Pomfret (Vt)

British Library Cataloguing in Publication Data

Goodenough, Simon
  The country parson.
  1. Church of England—Clergy
  I. Title
  262'.14   BX5175

  ISBN 0-7153-8238-1

Typeset by ABM Typographics, Hull
and printed in Great Britain
by Redwood Burn Limited, Trowbridge, Wilts
for David & Charles (Publishers) Limited
Brunel House   Newton Abbot   Devon

Published in the United States of America
by David & Charles Inc
North Pomfret   Vermont 05053   USA

CONTENTS

To the memory of
my great-great-great-great-grandfather
William Goodenough
Rector of Broughton Poggs
in the County of Oxfordshire
and his son
Samuel
Bishop of Carlisle
and his son
Edmund
Dean of Wells
also to my children's grandfather
Rector of Upton Pyne and Vicar of Brampford Speke
in the County of Devonshire

1
THE PARSON

Parsons are very like other men, and neither the better nor
the worse for wearing a black gown.

Philip Stanhope, Earl of Chesterfield

And sometimes comes she with a tithe-pig's tail,
Tickling a parson's nose as a' lies asleep,
Then dreams he of another benefice.

Romeo and Juliet, William Shakespeare

As a body of men, parsons have been so put upon, so much the
butt of humour and derision, so often warmly loved and warmly
hated, that it is difficult to paint them in unexaggerated colours.
We laugh at the parson but he is not contemptible; we protest
when his authority rises too high or when his weakness trips him
up, but he exists both as a leader and as a fellow sufferer at our
own invitation; he comes unfitted for the task and yet we bow
to his experience. So many epithets are directed at the man:
pastor or parasite; oppressor, teacher, friend or fool. But
however long the list, the catalogue of human character is
inexhaustible. All we can do is simply patch him together with a
medley of memories, some of them his own, some those of his
friends and enemies.

It seems only fair to give him a good start, with the sound
approval of no less a critic of mankind than Geoffrey Chaucer,
one of the greatest champions of the country parson. The poet
first has some sharp words to say about the far less savoury
nature of the parson's fellow churchmen, for there were several
men of God among that chattering company on the pilgrim road
to Canterbury during those April days toward the end of the
fourteenth century. Beside the entourage of the blameless

9

prioress, Eglantine, and the parson himself, there were a monk, a friar and a pardoner.

The monk loved fine clothes, swift greyhounds and a fat roast swan better than books and the cloister. He was a self-confessed 'prikasour', a horseman who did not give a plucked hen for the rule that hunters are not holy men. The venal friar, who earned his beer money by granting easy absolution, was no better. He would have rather passed the day in the company of alehouse men than among lepers and beggars. As for the hypocrite pardoner, with his shoulder-length, flaxen hair, his beardless, gelding chin, his feigned flattery, relics, ostentatious singing and smooth-tongued preaching, he would earn more in one day than the parson could earn in two months.

The parson was stamped from a different mould: a good man, poor in pocket but rich in thoughts and deeds; patient, diligent and kind; who would rather give to his people than take tithes; who walked throughout his parish to visit the sick, whatever their rank, whatever the weather; who led his flock by example first and only then by preaching. His maxim was simple:

> If gold ruste, what shal iren do?
> For if a preest be foul, on whom we trust,
> No wonder is a lewed man to ruste.

Chaucer's Parson, copied from the Ellesmere manuscript (*Mansell Collection*)

THE PARSON

Chaucer's contemporaries did not all agree with the poet's conclusion, that 'a bettre man I trowe that nowher noon ys'; they kept the purple of their phrases for more licentious goings-on. Critics preferred to lump the local priest in with all the other ranks of the regular and secular clergy, whom they felt were to blame for the laxness of the age. The monk, the friar, the pardoner, the parson and even the prioress were believed jointly to be responsible for the errors and scandals that had apparently become established forms of church behaviour. Already there were those who looked back to the Saxon origins of the country parson for an ideal lost to greed, privilege and mediocrity.

The Christian message first spread through the scattered communities of rural Britain in the wake of St Augustine's evangelising mission of AD 597. Itinerant priests and monks set out through each kingdom from the bishop's 'minster' to preach from stone or wooden crosses set up at crossroads and other public places. Their regular visits soon became a welcome part of the village scene. That venerable historian, Bede, was full of admiration for their activities and described with satisfaction how the people ran out to greet the preachers, receiving them joyfully, bowing to them and begging to be blessed by them. Being a monk himself, Bede wrote with a rose-tipped quill of the kind concern the preachers had for the people's good. He shrugged off any hint that avaricious thoughts might lead his colleagues to hope for land or money in reward.

Land and money certainly came but at first only as much as the job was worth. Local lords showed spontaneous interest in the activities of the preachers and sought to harness them to the purpose of social order. In establishing the skeleton of a parochial system, they were greatly encouraged by Archbishop Theodore. The lords provided for the building of the churches, appointed a priest as rector and supplied him with a benefice of glebe land for his support. Churches were founded and parsons put in wherever communities required them and landlords saw fit to endow them. The first parishes were large but soon broke down, as new land was cleared and new villages within the old parish required their own churches and rectors.

11

Consecration of a Saxon church, from the Cotton manuscript (*Mansell Collection*)

The system spread quickly. By late Saxon times, the village church was looked on as the centre of community life and the rector had assumed responsibility for the general welfare of his flock beyond simply the care of their souls. He preached to them only rarely but conducted regular services in Latin; he visited the sick and relieved the poor with the profits of the church's tithes; he heard confession and often arbitrated in disputes between neighbours; he was friend and guide and fellow farmer to the whole community, as well as their bulwark against medieval fears of hell and damnation; he was also, at times, their champion against an oppressive landlord. Sometimes the rector was the younger brother of the landlord but in general he was no better off than the majority of his parishioners and often he was barely more literate than they were. His influence, even so, was on the whole for good. Such errors as he was susceptible to were chiefly personal. It was not until the Norman Conquest that the system itself became distorted by outside interest in the golden opportunities it offered.

The Conquest upset the rural calm and sowed the seeds of great disturbance in the careful balance of community life around the church. The new Norman lords, brought up closer to the influence of Rome than their Saxon counterparts, gave their support to the monasteries and thus effected invidious changes in the parochial system. The advowson, or right to present a priest of his own choice to the benefice, often passed from the Saxon landlord to his Norman successor when the latter seized possession of the manor. The Norman might then, by a procedure known as appropriation, vest the rectory in a local monastery in exchange for political favours or for prayers on behalf of his soul.

So the monastery became rector, entitled to the profits of the tithes and glebe land but, being a corporate rector, it could not perform the personal ministerial duties required in a cure of souls; it therefore had to appoint a vicar to carry out those duties 'vicariously'. When Henry VIII dissolved the monasteries in 1536–9, many rectories passed into the royal hands and were granted to laymen. The right to the profits was said to be 'impropriated' by the lay rector. Being lay, he too had to appoint a vicar.

Whether the rector was a monastery or a layman, the vicar was far too often paid a miserable stipend. This prompted him to increase his income by acquiring more than one benefice. The more parishes an underpaid and overworked vicar adopted, the less likely he was to serve any of them properly, and so he in turn appointed a chaplain or curate to oversee each at an even lower stipend than he himself was receiving from the rector.

This process was mirrored in the conduct of many of the

13

The Orthodox true Minifter,

Church and Conventicle, from a tract of 1641, titled 'A Glasse for the Times'
(*Mansell Collection*)

proper, functioning rectors; that is, the incumbents of those rectories which had been neither appropriated nor impropriated. These men increased *their* incomes by acquiring further benefices but, since they, unlike the vicars, were entitled in the first instance to the full emoluments of the rectory, their motive tended to be greed rather than economic necessity. Sometimes this aggrandisement was facilitated by the sinecure rectory, where the rector was relieved from residence and had no spiritual duties (he was 'without cure'), these being executed by a vicar. Of course, there were rectors who behaved with much more responsibility towards their duties.

One way and another, it soon became impossible to disentangle the complexities of the system. The absentee rector and the pluralist vicar had both become part of an intricate labyrinth of self-interest in which every parish was innocently trapped for the next 700 or 800 years. These twin scandals, with their attendant vices, quickly became fair marks for every form of criticism, but they evaded all the feeble attempts at reform from the twelfth to the nineteenth centuries. They did much to shape social attitudes adversely during that time and to influence the welfare of rural communities. They highlighted the irresponsibility of the Church in failing to set its own house in order before preaching on the behaviour of the people it purported to serve. These were no pleasant human weaknesses but the product of a permitted system of landed interest. The absentee and the pluralist together form the Achilles heel of our story.

Not all absentee rectors and vicars were necessarily evil or lax. Many were absent on official business for an ecclesiastical or lay master; some were performing duties as household chaplains; others were attending universities, with special dispensations from Rome. In such cases, the absentee was supposed to appoint a chaplain or curate to care for the parish in his stead. The parish was often better served by the chaplain than it had been by the absentee. Permission for absence was also granted for those who wished to go on pilgrimage or to attend the obsequies of some important prelate, but the time allowed was not always generous. The vicar of Brixham was granted only ten weeks to visit Rome in 1308 and was threatened with dismissal if he came back late. Another Devon vicar enjoyed a far more leisurely sabbatical: he was given a year's leave merely to attend the obsequies of William of Wykeham. All these men, the rectors, the vicars and the curates, can be called 'parson'. The term is often loosely applied to all clergymen, but strictly it should be confined to incumbents of a benefice.

There was more blame than praise to be heard of the country parson in the centuries leading up to the Reformation. Chaucer's voice of approval was a lone one. The fourteenth-century poet William Langland thought it scandalous that low-born bondsmen and beggars were becoming priests, although most wealthy families had a parson son. John Wyclif, rector of Lutterworth, who died in 1384, jibbed at the payment of tithes to non-residents. The privileges of the church courts were under attack. Absentee parsons were accused of chasing mistresses, drink or plain profit. The parson himself was none too happy, living in dread of his bishop's or archdeacon's visitations, whose princely retinues ate him out of glebe and tithe. His simplicity was mocked by more sophisticated monks and he watched with irritation while travelling friars stole his congregation for their flamboyant preaching on the village green.

It was an easy matter to exploit anti-clerical feeling in the country in support of the Reformation and the dissolution of the monasteries. In the wake of the political nationalism that had spread through Europe, the influence of Rome had become intolerable and a flood of new Protestant ideas was pouring out of the universities. Colet, Tyndale and More joined the outcry against Church abuses. The books to read were the *De Imitatione Christi* of Thomas à Kempis, English translations of Sebastian Brant's *Narrenschiff* or *Ship of Fools*, Erasmus' *The Praise of Folly* and *Manual of a Christian Soldier* which laid great empasis on the study of Christ's life and the Bible. Torn away from Rome, the Church immediately became more personal, based once more on the scriptures themselves and not so much on symbols, rituals and mystery.

The trappings of Rome were cast off. The churches were

stripped of their wealth. An English Bible was placed in every church and the priest abandoned his place of eminence in the distant chancel, moved down toward the nave, turned to face his congregation and addressed them at last in their own tongue. Thomas Cranmer became the first Protestant Archbishop of Canterbury in 1533. The following year, King Henry VIII became the supreme head of the Church of England. Two years later, Thomas Cromwell, as Vicar-General, exercised the new royal supremacy against the scandals in the monasteries. Buildings were plundered and closed down. Abbots and monks were thrown out, though their sufferings were eased by generous compensation. Many abbots were content to become the parson of the parish from which they had once milked all the profit. Few of the evictions were attended by the sort of hardship experienced by the Royalist clergy at the hands of the Puritans a century later.

The average country parson weathered the official change of attitude with reasonable ease, provided he was sensible of his own safety and watched the political barometer warily. In the Shropshire village of Myddle, the transition was made with relative calm, according to Richard Gough, who wrote up his history of the parish more than 150 years later. Mr Thomas Wilton was the first rector of Myddle after the Reformation and remained there for many years: 'He was careful to Reforme those things, that through negligence, were grown into disorder, and to settle things in such a way as might conduce to the future peace and benefit of the parishioners.'

Others found the 1549 Act of Uniformity and Cranmer's New Prayer Book more than they could stomach. There were uprisings in Norfolk and the South-West. One sparking point for the so-called Prayer Book Rebellion was in the small Devon village of Sampford Courtenay, where there was an immediate protest against the royal proclamation that on Whitsunday, 10 June, all clergy should celebrate divine service according to the English rite of the First Prayer Book of Edward VI. William Harper, rector of Sampford Courtenay, quietly did as he was bid, like many other practical men, but the villagers were in no mood to tolerate new-fangled ways. Thomas Underhill, the tailor, and

William Syms, a labourer, acting as spokesmen for the congregation, called the new English Prayer Book a 'foolery' and a
'Christmas mumming play'. They demanded the reinstatement of
the old Mass and the restoration of statues and pictures of Mary,
Jesus and the saints. Harper succumbed to their threats and
reverted to the Latin service but that was not the end of the
affair. Local indignation spread. Parishioners throughout the
South-West were furious that their traditional beliefs and forms
of worship were being undermined. There were riots, which
spread to Exeter and were cruelly suppressed by the king's men.
Many ill-armed countrymen were slaughtered.

Harper himself survived but a fellow parson was hung for
siding with the rebels. The vicar of St Thomas, Exeter, was
Robert Welshe, a tough woodsman with a reputation as a good
wrestler and a fine shot, 'such a one as would not give his head
for the polling, nor his beard for the washing'. This capable and
courteous man of God became 'an arch captain and a principal
doer' among the rebels in their attempted siege of Exeter and
it was he who ordered that a messenger be hung who was found
carrying letters from the city to the king's commander, Lord
Russell. The hanging took place on Exe Island, a calculated
insult to the king since the island was Crown property. Welshe
was not carried away by the novelty of violence. When the
majority of the rebels wanted to fire the city, it was he alone
who stopped them 'from enterprizing so wicked a fact'. He
got no thanks for this good deed. When Lord Russell raised
the siege, the vicar was bound in chains, wearing his Roman
vestments, and strung up on a gallows on the tower of his own
church. It is recorded that he died very slowly.

Four years later, Edward VI was also dead and Queen Mary
brought back all things Roman, to the delight of some and the
confusion of many. Five years on and Mary, too, was dead.
Elizabeth rejected Rome once more. The country parson struggled
to follow these bewildering changes and prayed that, if occasionally he tripped, his congregation, equally at sea, would fail to
notice or report him.

He did not escape censure altogether. The Archbishop of

York found much to complain about in the behaviour of his country clergy during the first years of Elizabeth's reign. One rector was so drunk that he could not even say the service; another was seen to wear a sword at his side and was known to be a 'notable fornicator'; a third brewed ale in the vicarage with the help of his brother and sold it to his friends; a fourth had a quick temper and galloped through the service so fast that the congregation could not follow what he was saying; a fifth was non-resident, failed to redistribute the profits of his benefice to the poor and gave no instruction to the parish children in their catechism. Other dioceses no doubt had similar problems: few were incurably dreadful and none differed much from the general run of complaints that persisted for the next two centuries.

There was a general tightening up of the Church and of society during Elizabeth's reign. Educational standards were raised as well as moral ones. More clergymen passed through the increased number of Tudor grammar schools and Archbishop Grindal insisted that every clergyman should study the scriptures and read at least one chapter of both the Old and the New Testament every day. The Sabbath became increasingly a special holy day of rest. It was forbidden to sell liquor in taverns during Sunday service, which the people were compelled to attend by the threat of a shilling fine if they failed to do so. Approved clergymen only were permitted to preach freely; the majority used the twenty-or-so licensed texts provided by the authorities.

The popular image of the free-wheeling Elizabethan entrepreneur should be balanced by noting the authoritarian strait-jacket fitted tightly over the country. The parson himself became a part of the state system and shared with the local constable some of the responsibility for supervising the movement of people across parish boundaries. No villager could leave his parish without a testimonial from the constable and the incumbent, who together kept a careful eye on the three or four million vagabonds and rogues that plagued the countryside during Elizabeth's 'glorious' reign. In some parishes, the parson himself was increasingly subjected to the whim of his patron, quite probably an upstart bourgeois gentleman who had profited from the redistribution of land and rectories after the dissolution of the monasteries and who was eager to steal a share of the lucrative simoniacal profits to be made by trading in benefices. In other parishes, an absent or disinterested landlord often left the parson master of his own fate and that of his parishioners.

The Puritan and the Catholic were not always left in peace quite so readily, though persecutions of the Catholics only occurred at times of crisis. A Catholic uprising against the Anglican form of service, in November 1569, under the Earls of Westmorland and Northumberland, failed through lack of popular support. A purge of Catholic priests after the Armada scare saw almost sixty dead. Many Catholic chaplains continued to serve their masters discreetly in the fashion of the Old Faith and caused no outward disturbance.

The Puritans, on the other hand, were eager to be recognised and grew noticeably stronger toward the end of the 1580s. There were between 300 and 400 Puritan ministers in the country by the end of the century. Enthusiastic preachers, they urged a ban on Sunday social activities, rejection of all ornament, close study of the Bible, extempore prayers and communal psalm singing. They attacked plural livings vigorously and regarded as quite inadequate Elizabeth's Canons against the holding of more than two benefices simultaneously. Not so many years later, they found this particular hobby-horse easier to ride in the pulpit than in practice.

Their support in the country was as much political as religious, for they won sympathy and benefices from many of the new landowners in the House of Commons. Occasionally, Elizabeth found it necessary to make an example from among the Puritans to keep them in order. John Greenwood and Henry Barrow were both hanged in 1593, after being in prison for six years for refusing to conform to Archbishop Whitgift's Twenty-four Articles of 1584. Any clergyman suspected of questioning Royal Supremacy and Church authority was required to answer the articles on oath. More than 300 clergymen refused to do so. Puritan John Udal died in prison in 1591, after publishing *A Demonstration of Discipline*, which denounced Elizabeth's bishops.

The tempo of Puritan protest increased after the queen's death, as religious tensions suppressed during her reign began to break out. Extremist Calvinists and Evangelicals joined the chorus, first against James and then against Charles and his High Church ally, Archbishop Laud. The political nature of the confrontation became increasingly apparent: Parliament and the rising gentry class fought for power against the central authority of the king and his bishops. It was a battle in which the country parson was inextricably caught up, whatever his beliefs. The Puritans were the first to suffer as the king hastily clamped down on their activities and evicted the more extreme. With the appointment of Laud as Archbishop in 1633 and the implementation of his policy of 'Thorough' elimination of Calvinist and Puritan opposition, events took on a crueller turn. Laud's dreaded Visitations resulted in ears cut off, noses slit, faces branded, fines, whippings and imprisonment. It looked to many like the threat of a return to Rome. Nonconformist protest was transformed into fanatical opposition to the policies of the king.

While the plot of this drama was developing in the political foreground, Puritans and Anglicans had little choice but to settle for coexistence in most parts of the country. The situation was not particularly comfortable for the Anglican incumbent but it was not necessarily intolerable. The Puritan refusal to stick to the rules was more of an irritant than a real threat. Puritan members of the congregation kept their hats on in church; they refused to stand to say the Creed or to bow at the name of Jesus; they objected to the sign of the cross at baptism, to wedding rings, to the churching of their wives after giving birth, to the parson's surplice, his cassock and his university hood. The churchwardens, who were supposed to keep the congregation in order, frequently turned a blind eye to Puritan defiance, for they often secretly supported the Noncomformists. The parson could do little more than order the height of the pews to be lowered, so that he might keep a closer eye on his wayward flock. Outside his own church, he was powerless to prevent the Puritans from holding their own meetings, instituting their own lay elders and deacons or giving sermons in their own houses.

Despite the troubled times, there were men of peace and goodwill on both sides. The Elizabethan parish could boast such fine examples of the traditionally caring parson as William Harrison of Radwinter, who left his money to the poor of his parish, and Richard Hooker of Bishop's Bourne, a humble but brilliant scholar who, despite a shrewish wife, lived an exemplary life and wrote *Of the Laws of Ecclesiastical Politie*, (1594–7), which underlined the Elizabethan Settlement. There was also the justly famous Parson Gilpin of Houghton-le-Spring, the 'Apostle of the North', who kept open board on Sundays, returned the tithes of the poor and refused a bishopric. 'Father Gilpin,' said his bishop, 'I acknowledge that you are fitter to be the Bishop of Durham than I am to be parson of your church.'

There were reasonable and moderate Puritans in the following century: men like Richard Baxter (1615–91), who was genuinely disturbed by the excesses and failures of his Anglican colleagues; men like Hugh Clark, vicar of Oundle, who turned his congregation away from their Whitsun Ales and their ungodly dancing by gentle admonishment and by the example of his own life. One young hot-head, angered by Clark's attitude, went to stab him in the street but Clark talked to him, dissuaded him and won the man's support. Equally, there were caring, High Church parsons, like George Herbert (1593–1633), who abandoned the chance of a glittering career at court to become an ordinary country parson according to the lawful Anglican ceremonies.

Good men and goodwill were sadly not enough to keep the peace for long. Parliament reassembled, in 1640, after eleven years of personal rule by King Charles. Laud was impeached and the House of Commons ordered churchwardens throughout the land to remove communion rails, level chancels, strip down crucifixes, candles and all forms of ornament. The Book of Common Prayer was abolished in 1645 and replaced by a Directory of Public Worship. The king himself was executed in 1649 and the monarchy abolished. Justices of the Peace took over the duties of the Church courts and the archdeacon's visitations. Out of a total of 8,600 incumbents, throughout the country, some 2,425 Anglican clergy were evicted and replaced by an assortment of Presbyterian, Independent and Baptist 'intruders', as they were known, who took up the reins of the parish with little change. Most of the evictions involved force and subsequently great hardship. Those Anglican clergy who remained in their parishes learnt to keep their mouths shut and to conform with the new order.

The Puritans gave what seemed to them good reasons for the evictions. Pluralism headed the list; politics and immorality were close seconds. One parson was thrown out for 'sending a good horse to serve his Majesty, and a bad one to serve Parliament'. 'Dumb ministers', who did not preach, were sent packing. Accusations of immorality were difficult to disprove: incontinency with women, drunkenness during services, frequenting alehouses, fighting and gambling, were all cited against them. One parson was accused of gluttony, for 'eating custard publicly – and with great greediness'.

If it is true, as Swift said later, that 'nothing can render the clergy popular but a degree of persecution', then the Anglican clergy were already heading for a return to favour. Their sufferings during the Commonwealth were very real, sometimes tragic and often entertaining. Drawing chiefly on original letters, the Reverend J. Walker compiled an account of the *Sufferings of the Clergy in the Times of the Late Rebellion*, which he published sixty years later, in 1714. This account provides many of the best tales of those experiences.

The case of the elderly Richard Reynolds, rector of Stoke Fleming, spanned the changing fortunes of the period. Reynolds fled from his home disguised as a farmer, and met Cromwell's soldiers as they came to seize him. The soldiers asked the anonymous farmer the way to Stoke Fleming and he pointed it out, adding mischievously that he hoped they would catch 'that old malignant Reynolds'. He fled to Cornwall, until his wife paid £100 protection money for him to return to his parish, where for a time he was forced to have Puritan soldiers billeted in the rectory. He was eventually evicted for a second time; he was then supported by his daughter's spinning and finally returned to Stoke Fleming at the time of the Restoration, at which point, thoroughly worn out, he resigned in favour of his son-in-law.

Boldness, ingenuity, defiance and common sense were the requirements for survival. Peter Grigg, curate of Churston Ferrers, calmly recited the Lord's Prayer while a Puritan soldier put a pistol to his head and tried to stop him. 'I have done my duty as a minister,' said Grigg, when he had finished his prayer, 'now you can do what you think is your duty as a soldier.' The man was shamed into sparing Grigg's life. Another Anglican played on the sympathies of the soldiers by gathering all his neighbours' children into his run-down parsonage and pleading poverty and the size of his family as a good reason to be left in peace.

Some who tried to escape were less successful than old Reynolds. One royalist sympathiser ruptured himself when clambering over the rectory wall. A second broke his thigh when struggling through a priest-hole into a neighbour's house. William Lane, rector of Ringmore, hid in his own church tower, after leading his parishioners in a fruitless fight against the Roundheads. He was forced to remain there for three months before he escaped, listening each Sunday to the rantings below him of the intruding minister preaching from his own pulpit. Other Anglicans did not escape at all. Many were put in prison hulks, with the unfulfilled intention of sending them as slaves to plantations or to Algiers. Amias Hext, rector of Badcary, was in prison for a year and drew up a list of complaints against the Puritans: 'In this confinement, I am debarred of seven things dear to me:

1. The society and company of my wife
2. The company and comfort of my children
3. The fellowship and comfort of my parishioners
4. The want of the benefit of my living
5. The restraint and exercise of my function
6. The abridgement of my liberty
7. The want and use of my books.'

Some parsons, like James Forbes of Bovey Tracey, went out only under the strongest protest. Forbes was finally ejected from his living and fined £30. 'I will lend it to buy halters to hang them all,' he declared and took care to hide the brass eagle and lectern until he could restore them to his church after the Restoration. The intruding minister, Tucker, thought it wise to preach with a sword by his side and attempted but failed to saw the font in half.

Other parsons submitted meekly but won their revenge in due course. Joseph Barnes was evicted, together with his seven children, from the parish of East Ilsley. The intruding minister, John Francis, refused to pay Barnes compensation of one-fifth of the value of the living as ordered by the Puritan committees, even when Barnes sent his youngest daughter to beg for the money. Shrugging his shoulders and sighing, Barnes accepted that 'starving is as near a way to heaven as any other', but he regained his living at the Restoration and Francis fled the country to avoid being forced to pay the arrears he owed to the proper incumbent.

Dr Turner of Fetcham was turned out of his rectory in equally unfortunate circumstances but also lived to see his position dramatically reversed. His wife was about to have a baby when the intruder, Fisher, arrived to take over. Fisher had no pity. The rector and his wife were at once evicted. By a curious turn of fate, Fisher's own wife was in a similar condition when Turner came back at the Restoration. 'You shall see I am a Christian,' said Turner. 'In the name of God, let her tarry and welcome.'

The rector of Chelmsford, John Michaelson, barely escaped with his life. He was standing at a graveside, conducting a burial from the Book of Common Prayer, when members of the congregation flung him into the grave and were about to bury him alive. He was only saved by the remonstrances of some of the older townsfolk. At another funeral, a curate suffered the minor indignity of having his surplice cut off. His rebellious congregation used also to ring the bells loudly whenever he attempted to lead the prayers in church.

For many Anglican parsons, survival was largely a matter of adapting to conditions and keeping out of trouble. One who found mental agility easier than physical escape, for he was a large man, was Thomas Fuller of Broadwindsor in Dorset. Fuller became famous for his *Church History of Britain*, which was published posthumously in 1662. Although his sympathies lay largely with the Royalists, he deftly managed to remain on reasonable terms with the Parliamentarians. Once, when being questioned closely as to his beliefs and allegiance, he quipped cheerfully to his interrogator: 'Sir, you may observe that I am a pretty corpulent man, and I am to go through a passage that is very straight: I beg you would be so good as to give me a shove and help me through.' Fuller survived the Commonwealth without much hardship but died suddenly soon after.

Loyal Anglican congregations often supported their parsons in hiding and withheld their tithes from intruding ministers, but undoubtedly many intruders gained the affection of their new parishioners and sometimes they were more humane and approachable than the regular incumbents. It was, moreover, not only the resident Anglican clergy who suffered from the activities of soldiers during the Civil War years. Resident Nonconformists suffered also.

There is the happy story of John Dod, vicar of Fawsley in Northamptonshire, a passive Nonconformist whose house was raided three times by the Royalists. The second time, they found him sick in bed and snatched the pillows and bed-curtains from where he lay. The third time, they found him sitting by the fire and left him there with a pile of plundered sheets while they looked round for more. Dod took great satisfaction in 'plundering the plunderers' and hid the best pair of sheets beneath his chair before the Royalists returned.

Reasonable, moderate dissenters like John Dod and Ralph Josselin of East Colne in Essex often found their loyalties stretched to breaking point by the extremist factions within their own party. Josselin actually stood up to Archbishop Laud and as a result was raided by the Royalists but the majority of his Anglican parishioners regarded him with affection and he himself welcomed the return of the monarchy. The eccentric activities of the Quakers drove him to droll criticism: 'Sad are the fits at

Coxal (Coggeshall),' he wrote, 'like the pow-wowing among the Indies.'

John Milton (1608–74) summed up another uncomfortable aspect of the new order: the stern authority wielded in the community by the lay elders, or presbyters. 'New Presbyter is but old Priest writ large,' he grumbled. His contemporary, Samuel Butler, extended this theme in 'Hudibras' (1663–78), a burlesque on the Parliamentary Party, written at the time of the Restoration:

> Presbytery does not translate
> The papacy to a free state,
> A commonwealth of popery,
> Where every village is a see
> As well as Rome, and must maintain
> A tithe-pig metropolitan;
> Where every presbyter and deacon
> Commands the keys for cheese and bacon;
> And every hamlet's governed
> By's holiness, the church's head,
> More haughty and severe in's place,
> Than Gregory and Boniface.

Not surprisingly, most people were quite ready for the return of the king in 1660, after the depressing failure of the Commonwealth to fulfil its promise of a brave new world and in view of the increasingly bizarre extravagances of extremist sects. Some intruding ministers, having won the confidence of their parishioners and the previous incumbent being dead, agreed to conform to the old order and remained in their places. In many other cases, the previous incumbent returned peacefully to his inheritance. Robert Clarke of Andover came back quietly to his old parish late one Saturday. He stayed the night with a friend and on Sunday morning, when the church was full, he made his entrance at the west door. Every eye was on him as he walked through the body of the church toward the reader's pew, where the intruder sat. 'Sir,' said Clarke, 'the King is come to his own and will reign alone, and I am come to my own too and will officiate without an assistant.' He then turned to the congregation and delivered an excellent sermon on the forgiveness of injuries, which apparently went down well with most of his listeners.

There followed a disturbing period of counterswing and bloodless revolution. A new Act of Uniformity, demanding allegiance to the king and the Church of England, came into force on St Bartholomew's Day, 24 August 1662. Some 2,000 Noncomformist clergy refused to comply with the Act and resigned or were evicted, though generally in circumstances less harsh than their predecessors had experienced. A Declaration of Indulgence was passed ten years later, which licensed some Nonconformists to officiate once again, but this did not conceal the High Church inclinations of the king and his bishops. Charles II died a Catholic and it quickly became apparent that his brother James was eager to lead the whole country back to Catholicism. This was more, even, than conservative-minded country parsons could tolerate. Parson Johnson, rector of Corringham in Essex, printed an anti-papist tract in 1686, entitled *An Humble and Hearty Address to all English Protestants in the Army*. He was sentenced to stand in the pillory and he received more than 300 strokes from a whip on his way from Newgate to Tyburn. Two years later, there was a popular revolution against James. William of Orange was called in to save the country from the old, feared threat of Rome.

At once, the new king brought in a Toleration Act, allowing freedom of worship to all dissenters who took the oaths of Allegiance and Supremacy. By the end of the century, more than 1,000 chapels and meeting houses had been built and more than 2,400 licences had been granted to Congregationalists, Baptists and Presbyterians. No longer could the Anglican parson hold absolute sway over his entire parish. Members of his congregation might legitimately attend a Nonconformist meeting house for Sunday service in preference to the parson's church.

The hero of the anonymous song, 'The Vicar of Bray', found no difficulty, of course, in 'steering with the new wind' of William, just as he had kept his place through the century's turmoils:

And this is the law that I'll maintain
Until my dying day, Sir,
That whatsoever king shall reign,
Still I'll be the vicar of Bray, Sir.

On the whole, however, even the humblest parishes found themselves caught up in the nation's violent experience. In the 1640s,
the rector of Myddle, Mr More, who was 'commended for an
excellent preacher and as much blamed for his too much parsi-
mony, or covetousnesse, and want of charity . . . a loyal subject
of King Charles the 1st', was thrown out by the forces of
Parliament and fled to London. Twenty men from Myddle and
two neighbouring villages went to fight for the king, and thirteen
of them were killed. Only a handful went to fight for Parliament
and only one of these was wounded. The dissenting minister was
Mr Richardson but he, in his turn, retired peacefully to live a
'pyouse life'. The new minister was a mixed blessing: Mr
Holloway 'was naturally addicted to passion, which hee vented
in some hasty expression, not suffering it to gangrene into malice.
Hee was easily persuaded to forgive injuries but wisely sus-
piciouse (for the future) of any one that had done him a dis-
kindnesse.' Perhaps Mr Holloway was not unjustified in his
suspicions.

His lot must surely have been better than that of another
'typical' parson, as described with some exaggeration by
Macaulay in the last quarter of the seventeenth century: 'With
his cure, he was expected to take a wife. . . . A waiting woman
was generally considered as the most suitable helpmate for a
parson. . . . As children multiplied and grew, the household
of the priest became more and more beggarly. Holes appeared
more and more plainly in the thatch of his parsonage and in his
single cassock. Often it was only by toiling on his glebe, by
feeding swine, and by loading dung carts that he could obtain
daily bread; nor did his utmost exertions always prevent the
bailiffs from taking his concordance and his inkstand in execution.
It was a white day on which he was admitted into the kitchen of a
great house, and regaled by the servants with cold meat and ale.

His children were brought up like the children of the neighbouring peasantry. His boys followed the plough and his girls went
out to service.'

There was clearly much work to be done by the country
parson in re-establishing his position and his reputation after the
trials and tribulations of past years. Even by the mid-seventeenth
century, the parson's stock had sunk alarmingly low in many
quarters. George Herbert's call was much-needed then and just as
necessary half a century later: 'The domestic servants of the King
of Heaven should be of the noblest families on Earth,' he wrote,
'and though the iniquity of the late times have made clergymen
meanly valued, and the sacred name of priest contemptible; yet
I will labour to make it honourable, by consecrating all my
learning, and all my poor abilities to advance the glory of that
God that gave them.'

The eighteenth century did not, unfortunately, see that glory
revealed in the behaviour of the country parson but it did see him
become more prosperous. A feeling of exhaustion spread
throughout the rural parishes after the alarums of the seventeenth
century. The pleasant lethargy of the parson was disrupted only
by the enthusiasm of the Methodists and then by the Evangelical
revival. The pages of the century's diarists were more concerned
with profit and loss, with floating nicely on the rising tide of
social acceptance, with hunting, shooting, fishing, drinking,
eating and conversation, than with their churches, which often
remained shut all week.

The better face of the typical eighteenth-century country
parson appears in the diaries of men like Parson Woodforde or
William Cole, or in honest fictional characters like Fielding's
Parson Adams or Goldsmith's vicar of Wakefield. 'The hero of
this piece', wrote Goldsmith, 'unites in himself the three
greatest characters upon earth; he is a priest, a husbandman and
the father of a family. He is drawn as ready to teach and ready
to obey; as simple in affluence and majestic in adversity.' The
poet William Cowper (1731–1800), himself the son of a rector,
was one who saw a completely different profile of the country
parson:

But, loose in morals, and in manners vain,
In conversation frivolous, in dress
Extreme, at once rapacious and profuse;
Frequent in park with lady at his side,
Ambling and prattling scandal as he goes;
But rare at home, and never at his books,
Or with his pen, save when he scrawls a card;
Constant at routs, familiar with a round
Of ladyships – a stranger to the poor;
Ambitious of preferment for its gold,
And well-prepar'd, by ignorance and sloth,
By infidelity and love of world,
To make God's work a sinecure; a slave
To his own pleasures and his patron's pride:
From such apostles, O ye mitred heads,
Preserve the church! and lay not careless hands
On skulls that cannot teach, and will not learn.

The agricultural revolution brought about by improved farming methods during the century increased the value of land and helped to swell the parson's income. The rift between the 'haves' and the 'have-nots' grew greater but, for once, the parson found himself more or less on the right side of the divide, though his curate invariably was not. The improved financial possibilities of the vocation attracted a wider class of candidates for ordination. The local squire began to consider sending his son into the church or marrying his daughter to a clergyman. This new alliance with the squire confirmed the parson's rising status but at times brought with it open competition. Joseph Addison described in the *Spectator*, in the second decade of the eighteenth century, how in one village: 'The parson is always at the squire, and the squire, to be revenged on the parson, never comes to church. The squire has made all his tenants atheists and tithe-stealers; while the parson instructs them every Sunday in the dignity of his order, and insinuates to them, almost in every sermon, that he is a better man than his patron. In short, matters are come to such an extremity that the squire has not said his prayers either in public or private this half year; and that the parson threatens him, if he does not mend his manners, to pray for him in the face of the whole congregation. . . . Feuds of this nature, though too frequent in the country, are very fatal to the ordinary people; who are so used to be dazzled with riches, that they pay as much deference to the understanding of a man of an estate, as of a man of learning; and are very hardly brought to regard any truth, how important soever it may be, that is preached to them, when they know that there are several men of five hundred a year who do not believe it.'

Credibility in spiritual matters was certainly not the parson's strong point during the eighteenth century. Spiritual invigoration had been feebly attempted at the end of the previous century, with Nonconformist hymns, charity schools, religious societies for the reformation of manners among young men, a society for the propagation of the gospel and Acts against swearing and profanity but none of this had greatly stirred the parson's conscience. It was hardly surprising, therefore, that the Methodists found a warm reception in many quarters. The Wesley brothers, John and Charles, were brought up under the strong influence of their mother Susannah and their parson father, Samuel. John Wesley held his first open-air reading in Bristol in 1739 and launched the first Methodist Conference in 1744. He died in 1791. Together with colourful characters like the saintly John Fletcher, the vigorous John Berridge and the emotional preacher George Whitfield, he and his brother fought back against apathy and self-interest, against gambling, drunkenness and tritely reasonable sermons carefully suited to county congregations. Their very enthusiasm won them converts on the one hand and enmity on the other. For a while, they enjoyed fashionable popularity. The Countess of Huntingdon, known mischievously as 'Pope Joan', sold her jewels to build chapels throughout the country and appointed Whitfield to be her private chaplain in 1748. The carriages of aristocrats gathered at her house.

Opposition came chiefly from the Anglican parsons, who greatly resented the Methodists. Ignoring parish boundaries, Methodist preachers travelled about the country, gathering audiences wherever they could and establishing local societies

BRADFORD ON AVON, FROM THE NORTH-EAST.

The Anglo-Saxon church at Bradford-on-Avon, Wiltshire, and the church and vicarage at Stratford St Mary, Suffolk, from T. C. Bolton's *Abbeys and Churches*, 1890 (*Eileen Tweedy*)

'The Parish Vestry' by Thomas Rowlandson, 1784 (*Victoria & Albert Museum*)

'By piety's due rites tis given
To hold communion with Heaven.'

From Rowlandson's drawings of the adventures of Dr Syntax (*Mansell Collection*)

without regard for the rights of the local incumbent. 'I look upon the whole world as my parish,' said John Wesley defiantly. Anglicans were quick to fight back. Wesley himself was once refused the sacrament by a drunken curate and forced to preach out in the churchyard. On another occasion, the curate of Shepton Mallet hired a gang of bullies to sing him down while he was attempting to preach. The pistol-toting, drink-loving George White, curate of Colne in Lancashire, organised a private army to defend the Church of England and attacked the supporters of John Wesley and William Grimshaw with clubs and stones. In Swift's words, it appeared only too true that 'We have just enough religion to make us hate one another, but not enough to make us love one another.'

Parson Cole struggled valiantly to come to terms with the disturbance caused by dissenters in his parish of Waterbeach. 'The grief of griefs is that the parish swarms with Methodists – look which way I will the same heresy stares me in the face. Yet such is my wretched condition that I am obliged to be more than ordinary civil to these enemies of the Church and clergy. Only think how that must mortify my High Church spirit.' His tolerance was spoiled by the reason for it, which was self-interest: 'As to the discipline of our Church, through the practices of the dissenters, is now so relaxed as to come to nothing, there is no parleying with your parishioners on any point of doctrine or discipline, for if you are stiff they will abstain from all ordinances, or go over to the dissenters.' Dr Johnson (1709–84) was able to observe a different facet of dissenting influence with better humour: the presence of women preachers. 'A woman's preaching is like a dog's walking on its hinder legs,' he noted wryly. 'It is not done well; but you are surprised to find it done at all.'

In time, the Methodists, like the Presbyterians, the Independents, the Baptists and the Quakers, after a period of great success, were tolerated because they seemed no longer a threat. It was only at the end of the eighteenth century, with the alarm of the French Revolution ringing across the Channel, that there were mob riots against any dissenters who seemed at all dangerous to the stability of the nation. The Methodists were weakened by their own emphasis on the breaking up of parish boundaries. The very foundations of Anglican influence were being challenged. Roused to action and inspired by the Methodist example, the less privileged elements among the Anglican parsons responded with their own spiritual revival. The Evangelical movement obeyed Anglican discipline but otherwise paralleled many of the better characteristics of Methodism: spontaneous conversions and gospel preaching; chastity, morality, hymns and hard work; the relief of the sick and the poor; clubs and societies, Sunday schools and weekday services.

Evangelicism did not change everything all at once. Many eighteenth-century attitudes survived for a long time. Charles Lamb, writing in the early nineteenth century, found it difficult to disentangle the 'gentleman' from the 'parson': 'that class of modest divines,' he explained, 'who affect to mix in equal proportions the gentleman, the scholar and the Christian; but, I know not how, the first ingredient is generally found to be the predominating dose in the composition.' Pluralism and absenteeism were still common. It was estimated by William Cobbett, at the turn of the century, that 332 incumbents held 1,496 parishes and that 500 other parsons held another 1,524 parishes. Out of 10,800 livings in the country, it was reckoned that more than 6,300 did not have resident incumbents. The example given to parishioners was not helped by the influx of officers into the ranks of the ordained as a result of the disbandment of soldiery after Waterloo. They may have led their soldiers to victory but they were less fitted to lead their flocks to salvation. Parliament seemed unable to discipline the clergy and, in 1831, twenty-one bishops voted against the Reform Bill. They failed to judge the mood of the nation. There were riots. The following year, the bill was passed.

'Whenever you meet a clergyman of my age,' joked the ageing Sydney Smith to Gladstone in 1835, 'you may be sure he is a bad clergyman.' He could, at last, afford to joke on such a subject. The spirit of reform saved the Church from its slide into disrepute. The Oxford Movement (initiated in 1833) and the Christian Socialists, men like Bishop Samuel Wilberforce,

Charles Kingsley and the eccentric Parson Hawker of Morwenstow, revived the Church's flagging energy. Kingsley had no
time for 'saintliness'. 'A poor, pitiful thing,' he called it, 'not
God's ideal of a man but an effeminate, shaveling ideal.' He
favoured the robust approach and the practical solution. Meanwhile Wilberforce dealt sharply and sweetly with foolish
parsons inadequate for their jobs. 'My lord,' wrote one indig-
nantly, 'my congregation are maligning me.' 'No one is maligning
you,' replied the bishop. The parson took this for reassurance
and showed the letter proudly as testimony to his character.

Churches were restored and thousands built, stuffed with box
pews and three-decker pulpits. Keble's *Christian Year* of poetry
achieved ninety-five editions between its publication in 1827 and
Keble's death In 1862. *Hymns Ancient and Modern* became a
national institution overnight in 1861. The country parson
interested himself in sanitation, social reform, working-men's
associations, schools and missions, but when he invited the
villagers for their annual tea party on the vicarage lawn he still
held separate functions for the labourers, the tradesmen and the
gentlemen farmers. The Victorian parson, awkwardly split
between his old alliance with the squire and his new alliance
with the common people, combined in his person a complex
mixture of innate conservatism, philanthropy, concern for social
welfare, capitalism, poverty and a desire to please.

This last was provoked by a sense of competition with the
revival of dissent. The Anglican parson had to offer more than his
rivals, to keep his congregation: more clubs and excursions,
more festivals, more real care. Villagers made the most of what
was on offer, regardless of their beliefs, as one parishioner
explained: 'We baptises with the Baptists and attends the
Methodists and buries with the Church. One cannot be too
particular when in bis'ness.' One parson who made haste to score
a point against the opposition was Benjamin Lovell, rector of
Milton in Surrey, who impressed a Methodist cobbler by reading
extracts in the original from a Hebrew Bible. When asked later by
a friend where he had learnt his Hebrew, he confessed that he
had merely gabbled nonsense. 'The Methodist did not know

that,' he said, 'and I have impressed upon him my superiority.'

Ralph Waldo Emerson (1803–82) did not see the Anglican
Church to be superior in anything: 'The curates are ill-paid, and
the prelates are overpaid,' he wrote. 'This abuse draws into the
church the children of the nobility, and other unfit persons,
who have a taste for expense. Thus a Bishop is only a surpliced
merchant. Through his lawn, I can see the bright buttons of the
shopman's coat glitter. . . . The Church at this moment is much
to be pitied. She has nothing left but possession.' Between the
two, the curate and the prelate, the Reverend Paget painted a
kinder portrait of the country parson in a book called *The Owlet
of Owlstone Edge* (1856): 'The parsons were the best and most
devoted priesthood on the face of the earth, the most blameless
in their lives, the most kind and generous, the most conscientious, the most thoroughly imbued with the truth of what they
teach, not the least learned nor the least painstaking.'

It was a glowing tribute but, towards the end of the nineteenth
century, the country parson was not so close to his people as
once he had been. The railway had broken down the isolation of
distant parishes, bringing new ideas and opportunities into the
villages and providing the means by which country people might
be enticed into the towns. The greater freedom to exchange
opinions led many clergymen to become more interested in
theology and dispute than in their parish. There was a marked
withdrawal of the parson from the practicalities of everyday life
into the sanctuary of his study. A flurry of Acts regarding
discipline, the sale of benefices and the collection of tithes, in the
final decade of the century, set the parson safely at arm's length
from the fear of controversy and left his life ordered and con-
trolled. Less and less remained, either in the parson or in his
church, to win back the faith of declining congregations.

It was not a promising start to a new and difficult age. Where
was Parson Hawker now, striding through the driving snow on a
stormy night in his wild Cornish parish to bring fuel and blankets
to his isolated flock? Where was he, clad in his claret-coloured
coat and flying tails over a blue jersey with a red cross knitted
on one side, with his brimless plum beaver pulled down over

his head, fishing boots above the knee and a yellow poncho when he rode his mule? For all his faults and favours, where was the leader, the father, the friend, as Hawker himself described the dying breed?

'Severed from all personal access to the master minds of their age and body, shut in by the barriers interposed by the rude rough roads of their county – their abode in wilds that were almost inaccessible – thus did the west country parson develop about middle life into an original mind and man, sole and absolute within his parish boundary, eccentric when compared with his brethren in civilized regions, but the Person, the somebody of consequence among his own people.'

2

PARSONS, CURATES AND PREFERMENT

The parson knows enough who knows a duke.

William Cowper

The cleric whose living depends on it will find no difficulty
in believing in the Resurrection.

Samuel Butler

Before the parson was able to become a man of consequence
among his own people, he had, of course, to obtain a parish for
himself. He had to get a job. The qualifications required of him
were a blend of education and training, involving the rigours of
advancement through a number of minor offices, great patience,
the ability to lobby and to flatter and the resources to deal in
simony. If he had this blend in full, or any one of its ingredients
in abundance, he stood a fair chance, provided he had luck as well.

Even in Saxon times, there were nobly born as well as serf-
born priests, trained mostly in the monastic schools, where they
learnt a rich mixture of grammar, rhetoric, metre, classics and
astronomy. After becoming in turn a doorkeeper, reader,
exorcist, acolyte, sub-deacon and deacon, the would-be parson
did not become a priest until the age of twenty-four or -five and
then only if he had the promise of a definite post or was sponsored
by some form of patrimony.

Standards slipped when Norman landlords handed out benefices
to reward loyal retainers or to anyone else who would pay the
landlord a handsome percentage for the privilege. There was no
need for much education if a parish could be won this way. In any
case, country priests were increasingly of peasant or yeoman
stock and received what education they had from the parson
himself. They never went near a university. Alexander Barclay

had such a poor opinion of priestly erudition that when he translated the *Ship of Fools* in 1508 he left the helm of that ship to the misguided hands of eight canons from Ottery St Mary. Even though the opportunities for education at schools and universities greatly expanded during the fifteenth and sixteenth centuries and fees were high, still only one-tenth to one-fifth of the clergy were graduates. It was one thing to get a good education if you lived in the town, quite another if you lived on the land.

Even so, education for the church opened the doors to many jobs. A doctorate in theology could lead to high civil office, to employment at court, in cathedrals and in private households, as well as to a country benefice or two. Carpenter described how clergy in the fifteenth century 'tired and sweated to obtain church dignities, one in the king's kitchen, another in a bishop's court and a third in the service of a temporal lord' but it was the fools on Barclay's ship who understood the real secret of success:

> For if one can flatter or bear hawke on his fist,
> He shall be made parson of Honiton or Clyst.

Once established in his parish, the artful and unscrupulous parson looked round for an impecunious curate as desperate for a job as he himself had been before he gained his benefice; in other words, someone who would be prepared to do the work for him for a stipend of about one-tenth of its real value, thus freeing the parson to enjoy the remaining nine-tenths of the revenue of the parish at leisure. Bishop Langham made his feelings clear on this subject at the Synod of Ely in 1364: 'We strictly prohibit any rector from making a bargain with his assistant priest of this kind: that besides his fixed stipend he may take offerings for anniversary Masses, etc., since such a bargain is a clear indication that the fixed stipend is too small.'

That did not stop the flood of candidates for exploitation, all eager to get a foot on the bottom rung of the ladder of promotion at whatever cost. Many larger parishes had several curates to help the parson in the ceremonies and duties of the church. They visited the sick, relieved the poor and instructed the young; they baptised, sang masses for the dead and read the gospel and epistle. Some became chantry priests, looking after private chapels and often running schools, busily trying to please both their master and the parson in the hope of preferment. All this they did for five pounds a year, with no security of tenure, easily dismissed at the whim of the parson and with faint hope of winning a parish for themselves eventually. They were also fair game for the harshest censure of the anti-clerical critics.

The Reformation was more concerned with the monasteries than with correcting the country parson but nonetheless it caused him some bother. The cost of purchasing a benefice from his greedy new lay patron went up and the value to the parson of the benefice went down. Fewer men could afford to buy the jobs or to hold them: 'wherefore', said William Harrison of Rad-winter (who died in 1593), 'the greatest part of the more excellent wits choose rather to imploy their studies unto physicke and the lawes, utterlie giving over the study of the scriptures, for feare least they should in time not get their bread by the same.' 'Not a few find fault with our thred-bare gownes,' continued Harrison in his description of Elizabethan England, 'as if not our patrones, but our wives were cause of our wo. But if it were knowne to all, that I knowe to have been performed of late in Essex, where a minister taking a benefice (of less than twentie pounds in the Queenes books) was forced to paie to his patrone twentie quarters of otes, ten quarters of wheat, and sixteene yeerelie of barleie, which he called hawkes meat; and another lett the like in farme to his patron for ten pounds by the yeere, which is well worth fortie at the least, the cause of our thred-bare gownes would easlie appeare; for such patrons doo scrape the wooll from our clokes.'

There were those, of course, still happy to have a job at any price, if they were given it by a patron in reward for service. Harrison explained how the patron profited from this seeming generosity. Many lay patrons, he wrote, 'doo bestow advowsons of benefices upon their bakers, butlers, cookes, good archers, and horsekeepers, insted of other recompense, for their long and faithful service which they imploie afterward unto their most advantage. . . . The very cause weavers, pedlars and glovers have been made ministers . . . for a glover or a tayler will be glad of an augmentation of eight or ten pound by the yere, and well contented that his patron shall have all the rest, so he may be sure of his pension.' Such men were quite unqualified. Archbishop Parker wrote to Bishop Grindal in 1560: 'Whereas, occasioned by the great want of ministers, we and you both, for tolerable supply thereof, have heretofore admitted into the ministry sundry artificers and others, not traded and brought up in learning, and, as it happened in a multitude some that were of base occupations.'

Whether it was the fault of lay patrons for giving away benefices to servants and flatterers or the fault of the Church authorities for admitting base occupations, it was generally agreed that more and more clergymen were unlearned. One other excuse for this was that far fewer ordinands were going through the universities since the dissolution of the monasteries. Monastic houses had invariably supported the poorer students and given them free lodging. Without that support, the students could not afford a university education. Not only were they unable to keep up with the rush of new titles off the printing presses but many could not even master the nuts and bolts of their own faith. Bishop Hooper vetted 311 clergymen in Gloucester in 1551 and discovered that 168 could not repeat the Ten Commandments accurately, ten could not recite the Articles of Faith and ten did not properly know the Lord's Prayer. No wonder the more eager, active Puritans appealed to the awakening minds of the Elizabethans.

The man who did not hold a benefice suffered even more than the parson in the years after the Reformation. There was a substantial cut in supporting jobs for curates and chaplains. Official insistence that pluralist parsons should employ a competent curate in their second benefice provided jobs for only a few of those thrown out of work. Many others gave up their calling, unable to survive on stipends that were often less than the pay of an agricultural labourer. These turned their hands to their old trades or learnt some new skill: farming, teaching, even inn-keeping. None of this did the reputation of the Church any good. What curates were left were subjected to the harsh criticism of the Puritans for their 'lewd example', their 'super-stitions of the old faith', their 'dauncing among light and youthful company' or their 'failure to read the threateninge against synners'. On only one point did the Puritans back the curates; that was the question of pluralities:

> Bigamy of steeples is a hanging matter,
> Each must have one and curates will grow fatter.

The curate's situation did not improve in the following century. Any young scholar who wanted to keep his job had to do as he was told. John Rous wrote 'The Scholler's Lament' in his diary for the year 1641:

> In to some country village
>   Nowe I must goe,
> Where neither tithe nor tillage
>   The greedy patron
>   And coached matron
> Sweare to the Church they owe;
> But if I preach and pray too on the suddaine,
> And confute the Pope too, extempore without studying,
> I've ten pounds a yeere, besides my Sunday pudding.
>   Alas, pore scholler!
>   Whether wilt thou goe?

In the same year, a pamphlet was published called *The Curates Conference*, in which two curates bemoaned their fate. One com-plained to the other that he earned half as much as his double-beneficed parson and had been told that if he did not like the situation then the parson would find someone else who did. The other replied that half of everything he earned was taken out of his wages by the parson's wife and spent to deck herself out with fancy clothes and ribbons. Together, they proposed a strike. All curates should for one month refuse to read any sermons or prayers. Both young men took great delight imagining the pluralist parson riding frantically from one parish to the next to conduct both services. Sadly, they did not have the courage to carry through their plan. One joined a ship as chaplain and sailed to the East Indies; the other became a preacher in a regiment of soldiers.

There was another side to the quarrel, of course. One parson complained bitterly that his curate called him 'jacksauce and welsheroge' and boasted to his neighbours that his, the curate's, servants were better men than the parson himself. Other parsons treated their curates with great consideration. One rector was careful to leave to his curates as many as possible of those services, such as marriages, baptisms and churchings, that brought in extra fees, so that the curates could pocket the much-needed surplus. These were exceptional cases. On the whole, the curate remained firmly under the oppressive thumb of the parson and was no better off in the eighteenth century than he had been in the seventeenth century. This was partly the fault of the universities, which were once again turning out more ordination candidates than the Church could satisfy. It was the perfect set-up for the parson to drive the hardest sort of bargain.

Macaulay pictured the youthful curate's sorry plight in the last quarter of the seventeenth century: 'A young Levite – such was the phrase then in use – might be had for his board, a small garret, and ten pounds a year, and might not only perform his own professional functions, might not only be the most patient of butts and listeners, might not only be always ready in fine weather for bowls, and in rainy weather for shovelboard, but might also save the expense of a gardener or a groom. . . . He was permitted to dine with the family; but he was expected to content himself with the plainest fare. He might fill himself with the corned beef and the carrots; but as soon as the tarts and the cheese-cakes made their appearance, he quitted his seat, and stood aloof till he was summoned to return thanks for the repast, from a greater part of which he had been excluded. . . . Perhaps after some years of service he was presented to a living sufficient to support him.'

Twenty years into the next century, Thomas Stockhouse

addressed a pamphlet to Edmund Gibson, the Bishop of London. The pamphlet was titled *The Miseries and Great Hardships of the Inferior Clergy in and about London*, but it could equally have described the country curate: 'Mighty rectors riding over the heads of their readers and curates; receiving them with an air of superiority that would better become a Persian Monarch than a Christian priest; breaking jests upon their poverty, and making themselves merry with their misfortunes; turning them among the herd of their servants, in to the kitchen, till dinner comes in, and then shewing them what a mighty favour it is that they are permitted to sit down at the lower end of the table among their betters; curtailing in the meanwhile their allowances, which are held only at the will of their lord; keeping them under the worst of torments, a merciless suspense, and perpetual incertitude of daily bread; then turning them out at a minute's warning, purely to show the arbitrariness of their sway; and if at any time they pretend to murmur or complain, persecuting them with fury and revenge, and calling in a superior power to crush them.'

The dining restrictions were a particularly sore point among curates and chaplains. The latter were often housed in the squire's mansion to act both as private parsons and as private tutors to the young heir. They were generally treated like servants. If they attended the family dinner, they were allowed to stay for only half the meal and were sent out before the dessert appeared, just as Macaulay's 'young Levite' had been sent from the table. It was considered too worldly a pleasure for them to enjoy the sweet course. One young 'Mess John' or 'trencher chaplain', as they were often called, who stayed firmly in his seat and tucked eagerly into his pudding was given a sharp warning by the butler; he ignored the warning and was dismissed. The poet George Crabbe (1754–1832) was for a while Mess John to the Duke of Rutland and suffered in like fashion.

Joseph Hall's collection of satires, *Virgidemiarum* (1597), contains a clear picture of a trencher chaplain:

> A gentle squire would gladly entertain
> Into his house some trencher-chappelain

Some willing man that might instruct his sons,
And that could stand to good conditions.
First that he lie upon the truckle bed,
While his young master lieth overhead;
Second, that he do on no default
Ever presume to sit above the salt;
Third, that he use all common courtesies,
Sit bare at meals, and one half rise and wait;
Last, that he never his young master beat,
But he must ask his mother to define
How many jerks she would his breech should line;
All these observed, he would contented be,
To give five markes and winter liverie.

William Jones, curate and diarist, bitterly agreed that even at the end of the eighteenth century most curates were little better than liveried servants. He wrote of parsons as 'master-men, who do their duty by proxy, haggling with poor curates, till they can find those who will starve with the fewest symptoms of discontent'. Jones greatly pitied those fellow curates who had 'no other prospect but of being "journeymen", "soles" not "upper leathers" . . . mere "understrappers" in the Church. A journeyman in almost any trade or business, even a bricklayer's labourer or the turner of a razor-grinder's wheel, all circumstances considered, is generally better paid than a stipendiary curate.'

These journeymen of the Church were more than likely to wear the soles of their own boots out quickly enough in the work to which they were set. Physical stamina was required as well as humility and tolerance in the face of exploitation. Left by his parson to cover a wide parish, the typical Sunday of a hardworking country curate was deftly summarised by Dean Swift:

I marched three miles through scorching sand,
With zeal in heart, and notes in hand;
I rode four more to Great St Mary,
Using four legs, when two were weary:
To three fair virgins I did tie men,

In the close bonds of pleasing Hymen;
I dipp'd two babes in holy water,
And purified their mother after.
Within an hour and eke a half,
I preached three congregations deaf; . . .
All this perform'd by Robert Hewit:
What mortal else could e'er go through it!

There were no rewards in the short term for all this labour, only a large family, poverty, ingratitude and ill-health, as Swift also pointed out. Indeed, even in the long term, the only real reward was death; a peaceful end in an early grave was more than many dared hope for:

Thy curate's place, thy fruitful wife,
Thy busy, drudging scene of life,
Thy insolent, illiterate vicar,
Thy want of all consoling liquor,
Thy threadbare gown, thy cassock rent,
Thy credit sunk, thy money spent,
Thy week made up of fasting days,
Thy grate unconscious of a blaze,
And to complete the other curses,
The quarterly demands of nurses,
Are ills you wisely wish to leave,
And fly for refuge to the grave.

The 'insolent, illiterate vicar' was the bane of every curate's life. There were rectors and vicars, in turn, who thought their curate worse than insolent. Fielding in *Amelia* (1751) noted that 'there is not in the universe a more ridiculous, nor a more contemptible animal than a proud clergyman', and the parson, Dr Harrison, added a certain colour to the sentiment when he observed with satisfaction that he had put down 'that saucy passion, pride' in his curate. John Hepworth, vicar of Harwood in Yorkshire, came to grief at the hands of a very upstart curate, who was already established in the parish. This man, William Cheldrey, tried to turn the congregation against the new vicar and at the same time became engaged to Hepworth's daughter. He refused to perform any catechising, which posed a problem for the vicar, who was partly deaf and therefore could not himself hear the children's answers properly. 'Alas! I would feign live in peace,' cried Hepworth in despair.

Many curates, lacking Cheldrey's brashness, were resigned to remain curates all their lives, partly because they had little hope of ever gaining a benefice and partly because in any case they could not afford the fees for promotion. Some became vagrants, earning whatever they could from marrying and baptising other vagrants 'behind the nearest hedge'. Some, as in the previous century, eked out their living with 'lawless' jobs, such as gambling or inn-keeping. The majority contented themselves with 'drudging in a curacy' all their life, as William Combe's simple, scholarly and henpecked character Dr Syntax, who first appeared in 1809, soon discovered. The 'weekly journeys' made round the parish by this curate were very similar to the 'mighty labours' performed by Swift's Robert Hewit.

If a curate really wished to rise above this drudgery, then he had to keep an ear close to the ground for the first whisper of a vacant parish. All influential people, including the Crown, were constantly being lobbied for preferment, either by indigent curates in search of their first living or by parsons in search of a further living. The whole business was a lottery, depending largely on luck and perseverance. William Bagshaw Stevens, headmaster of Repton, found this out for himself when he invoked the aid of his friend, Thomas Coutts the banker, in seeking a living in the 1790s. 'For some time to come I shall be a very Death-Watch among the Ancient Incumbents,' he wrote and then added hopefully, 'Winter with all its horrors is again come upon us. . . . How this will agree with the Ancient Incumbents I know not.' Stevens seemed greatly disappointed by a visit from one old parson on whose living he no doubt had his sights: 'Old Edward was here the other evening as blithe as a bird and as tight as a drum.'

Another man in search of a good living was William Bicker-staffe, a curate and schoolteacher, already aged fifty-eight.

Bickerstaffe, 'having more inclination to a church living than a wife', made a number of applications for help to influential friends and aquaintances but died three years later after failing to win the quiet retirement job for which he yearned. He won instead an obituary in the *Gentleman's Magazine* that indicated he had missed his chance only by a hair's breadth: 'His case had been lately laid before the Lord Chancellor, from whom there is reason to think some preferment would have been bestowed on him had he lived.'

The Reverend Edmund Keene had not wasted his time with such uncertain tactics as those of Stevens and Bickerstaffe but in 1740 had taken a short cut to a living near Durham by promising to marry the illegitimate daughter of his prospective patron. Keene got the living and jilted the girl. He then paid her a handsome sum of money in recompense, to preserve the favour of his patron.

The Bishop of Derry took matters into his own hands when it came to selecting candidates for preferment in his diocese. The curates had to race along the beach and the winners took the best livings. It was a perfect example of the chancy nature of advancement.

For those who stayed the course and were successful, the prizes, on the whole, were worth the effort. After Dean Swift's picture of the 'busy, drudging scene of life' enjoyed by the average curate before he flew 'for refuge to the grave', he painted another picture, much more rosy, of what life might be if things were different:

> But, now, should Fortune shift the scene,
> And make thy curateship a dean:
> Or some rich benefice provide,
> To pamper luxury and pride; . . .
> To shine where all the gay resort,
> At concerts, coffee-house or court . . .
> With plenteous meals and generous wine;
> Wouldst thou not wish, in so much ease,
> Thy years as numerous as thy days?

'Credulity, Superstition and Fanaticism: a Medley' by William Hogarth, 1762
(*Mansell Collection*)

'A Village Choir' by Thomas Webster (*Victoria & Albert Museum*)

Creeting St Mary choir, Suffolk, 1900 (*Museum of East Anglia, Stowmarket*)

It was a happy dream but, alas, it was for most no more than a dream. There were too many curates for too few jobs and this situation continued into the nineteenth century. So too did the curate's penury. The minimum stipend for a curate was increased to £80 a year in 1813 but there were still plenty of young men only too happy to take half that wage to start them off in employment. Even in the second half of the century, there were many who still existed on much less than £80 a year. It was hardly surprising, therefore, that the popular image of a curate was of someone who washed his own shirts and pressed his trousers by laying them between the pages of a great Bible on which he then sat.

Sydney Smith (1771–1845), city wit and country parson, deplored the curate's lot and prophesied a nation-wide rebellion that would be harshly crushed by placing all young rebels on the 'tread-pulpit', an imaginary but fearful instrument of torture. 'What bishops like best in their clergy is a dropping down deadness of manner,' said Smith. He could have said the same of parsons and their curates. 'A curate,' he wrote, 'there is something which excites compassion in the very name of curate! A learned man in a hovel, with sermons and saucepans, lexicons and bacon, Hebrew books and ragged children, good and patient; a comforter and a preacher; the first and purest pauper of the hamlet.'

Charlotte Brontë (1816–55) married a curate but did not agree with Smith's charitable view of the breed. She said curtly, describing another curate before her marriage, 'I think he must be like all the other curates I have seen and they seem to me a self-seeking, vain, empty race. At this blessed moment we have no less than three of them in Haworth parish – and there is not one to mend another. . . . I regard them, one and all, as highly uninteresting, narrow, and unattractive specimens of the coarser sex.'

Not all the ladies were quite so censorious. Many a curate touched a tender heart among his congregation. This talent could be nicely balanced by a marvellous ability to put the rest of the church to sleep, as this popular rhyme neatly relates:

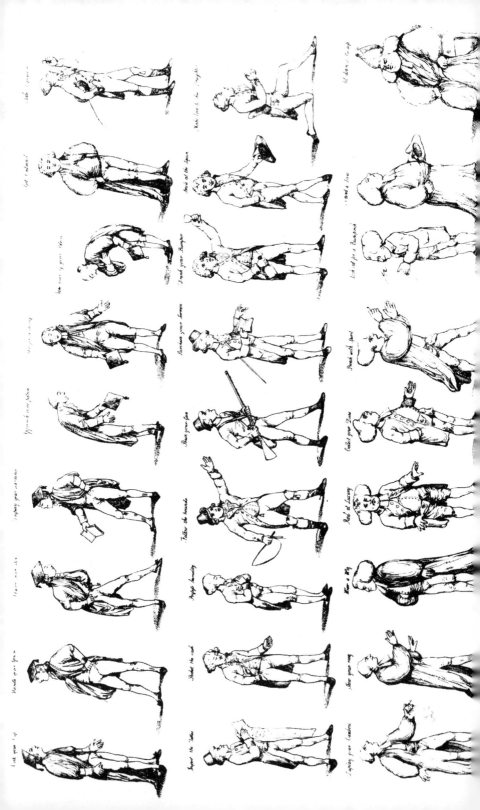

The ladies praise the curate's eyes –
I never see their light divine;
For when he prays he closes his,
And when he preaches closes mine.

Such gentle humour was not the style of Parson Froude of Knowstone in Devon, well known for eccentricity and a cruel sense of fun. Froude took a great dislike to one particular curate, got him drunk one Sunday, early in the day, and strung him up in a sack from a beam in a nearby barn. He then chastised the wretched man for failing to take the service he had missed. One equally hapless curate, in Cornwall, regarded by many as a 'harmless maniac', was firmly secured by a rope to the altar or reading desk during the service. It was reported that he earned extra money by playing his fiddle in the local inns

Strife continued at all levels between the curate and his parson during the nineteenth century. The parson tried to assert his authority and the curate tried to assert his independence. A docile curate still entered the rectory through the back door and gave an account of his expenses and his day's work to the rector's wife. An ambitious curate, on the other hand, could, if he tried, run rings around a feeble parson. The energetic, evangelical curate of St Peter, Mulworth, filled the church to overflowing when he took the service; it remained half empty when the parson preached. Not content with this success, the curate used to pray out loud, in front of the whole congregation, for 'his dear fellow labourer' and 'for the weak Shepherd at the head of the parish', much to the silent fury of the incumbent. The curate established a new church eventually and took with him a good proportion of his parson's flock.

But notable triumphs of this kind were rare. Like their eighteenth-century colleagues, most curates resigned themselves to bitterness and disappointment. Anthony Trollope (who died in 1882) described one such curate: 'Gradually there creeps

(Opposite) 'The Clerical Exercise' by Woodward, published in 1791 (British Museum)

55

upon him the heart-breaking disappointment of a soured and injured man. In the midst of this he takes to himself a wife . . . enjoying at the moment a little fitful gleam of short-lived worldly pleasure. . . . After that all collapses and he goes down into irrecoverable misery and distress. In a few years we know him as a beggar of old clothes, as a man whom from time to time his friends are asked to lift from unutterable depths by donations which no gentleman can take without a crushed spirit – as a pauper whom the poor around him know to be a pauper and will not, therefore, respect as a minister of their religion.'

This was the old man. For others, there was always hope, whatever the odds that history had proved against it. There was hope and there were the innocent country pleasures enjoyed by the gentle, passionate Francis Kilvert; pleasures that made the curate's work all worthwhile. Kilvert (1840–79) was curate to his own father and also to Parson Venables of Clyro in Radnorshire. His diary describes the delight he took in the sights and sounds of nature, in the people of the border parish, in gentle amusements. There were Valentines from 'Incognito', dances through the night ('I got to bed at 4.30 just as dawn was breaking'), bathing naked at Seaton on a hot July day. This last activity was something of an accident, though a happy one with no ill consequences. When he was undressing in his bathing hut, a boy brought him what he thought were two towels. Finding himself unprovided with a bathing suit of any kind, he bathed nude 'and set at nought the conventionalities of the place and scandalized the beach'. Too late, he discovered that one of the 'towels' was 'a pair of very short red and white striped drawers to cover my nakedness'. Although 'some little boys who were looking on at the rude naked man appeared to be much interested in the spectacle . . . the young ladies who were strolling near seemed to have no objection.'

He also enjoyed falling in love. To steal a kiss from a pretty girl brought him his greatest happiness: 'Shall I confess that I travelled ten miles today over the hills for a kiss, to kiss that child's sweet face. Ten miles for a kiss.' His worst problems were no more than a broken heart: 'I thought I was not going to care for any one again. I wonder if there is any receipt for hardening the heart and making it less impressible. I went sadly back to my room, took down and sorrowfully on with my sermon for tomorrow, feeling as if all was dull and blank and as if some light and interest had suddenly gone out of my life.' He married in 1879 and he died five weeks later, when he was not yet forty, not of a broken heart nor of the strain of duty but of peritonitis.

If, despite all these pleasures, frustrations and stumbling blocks, the average curate still had a mind to become a parson and had not the means nor the arrogance to thrust himself forward, he could still, in the nineteenth century, resort to the old and tried methods of flattery and fawning. Tennyson tried to catch the dialect of Spilsby in Yorkshire, with a description of the technique:

> But niver not speak paain out, if tha wants to git
> forrards a bit,
> But creeap along the hedge-bottoms, an' thou'll be
> a Bishop yit.

To have an uncle in high places was always useful, someone who could slip a young curate through his exams with painless ease and leave him ready and willing to take his place in a privileged world. No matter that the youth had a rather in-different degree from Oxbridge, provided he did not question the Bible and steered clear of Darwin. Archbishop Harcourt of York was able to ordain his nephew into the family living with small regard for the conventional pauses between steps on the ladder to promotion. 'I think it will save both you and me some trouble if I shoot through both barrels,' said the archbishop briskly, 'so I will ordain you both deacon and priest this afternoon.'

Once a parson had his own living, it was up to him to make the best of it. In some cases, he was his own squire as well, and there was no one he need fear. The nineteenth-century 'squarson' was a well-known figure, lord of both the manor and the rectory, holding the reins of authority in his village with absolute confidence. In other cases, the parson had still to be cautious with his patron, dine with him once a week, send him gifts from his garden, take care that he offered no offence from the pulpit.

Francis Kilvert one day watched a rare example of a different phenomenon, which occurred only after centuries of subservience and social climbing; he saw a parson even smarter than his squire – Parson Venables setting out from Clyro. 'It was refreshing to see the Vicar's stylish equipage driven by himself with two servants behind, dashing past the small humble turn-out of the Squire,' wrote Kilvert. He added that this was 'rather reversing the usual order of things' and we can note unconcealed admiration in his voice. If we did not already know him to be a sensible fellow, it would be easy to imagine that here he saw a symbol of the curate's eternal ambition.

3
THE PARSON AND HIS PURSE

An increasing family and a decreasing income. What is to be done?

William Jones, curate

The very word 'tithe' has ever been as unpleasing and odious, to farmers especially, as 'cuckoo' to the married ear. Those who pay them, pay them very partially, I may add 'grudgingly and of necessity'.

William Jones

The curate might have been more wary of the parson's job if he had known beforehand the uncertain nature of his income and the size of his outgoings. A great deal of the parson's time and energy was devoted to obtaining money and controlling his expenses. The means by which, over the centuries, he drew his income greatly influenced the character and attitudes of rural communities throughout Britain. His use or misuse of his income did much to determine the rise or fall of his popularity.

Among most communities, the parson's tithe, or tax of one-tenth, was an accepted fact of life, like any form of modern income tax. There was the usual grumbling when the time for payment came and the usual attempts to avoid or to reduce payment but in the end something always had to be paid. Times of stress between the parson and his parishioners occurred chiefly when the parson was blatantly abusing his income. Unfortunately for the parson, there were also times when community resentment stirred against an innocent man who was only trying to do his job, who found it hard enough to make ends meet and who loathed the task of demanding his dues from a reluctant community. Many parsons later used an agent for collection.

The early itinerant priests received some support from the monasteries which sent them out but they also relied on voluntary contributions from those who gathered to hear them preach. These contributions were chiefly in kind: a meal on the spur of the moment and something to put in their bag for the journey. The system became more structured when local landlords began to build their own churches and appoint their own priests. Together with the land for the church itself, the landlord set aside a portion of 'glebe' for the support of the priest. 'Glebe' literally means 'clod' or 'soil'. It was an area of farm and wood land, usually between thirty or forty acres, often scattered about the parish, held freehold by the priest to provide his subsistence.

Tied to the soil, the parson had to work as hard as any one of his parishioners, until successive generations of parsons found out that it was easier and more profitable to let their land than to farm it themselves. There were many who asked no more than a fair rent from smallholders anxious to enlarge their holding. There were others who demanded an extortive rent and got it from farmers desperate to find land at any cost on which to support themselves. Freed from the common toil that he had once shared, the parson distanced himself from the community.

The second source of the parson's income was his tithes. The tithe was the traditional scriptural payment of one-tenth of the produce of the land, of the creatures of the land and of a man's personal industry, due to God but payable to the rector as God's representative on earth and pastor of the flock (though it did nothing for the popularity of the tithe when this worthy justification was undermined after the dissolution of the monasteries by the appearance of lay rectors). This meant, for example, one-tenth of every harvest or one pig out of every litter of ten; but in many cases, to avoid the inconvenience of each parishioner paying his tithe in a variety of products, an agreement was made for the satisfaction of tithe by, say, the delivery of one-quarter of the hay instead of one-tenth of the produce of all the land, or the payment of a sum of money. And for personal tithes (of trades, fisheries and so on) only the tenth part of the clear profits would be due.

Whereas the glebe was provided by the landlord, the payment of tithe was dictated by the Church. The original intention behind it was not to increase the income of the parson but to enable him to redistribute the profits of the community among its poorer members. Produce was stored in the tithe barn and handed out as necessary. The temptation for the parson to regard an ever larger part of this supply as his private property was, not unnaturally, a very great one. Tithes were in fact voluntary in many parts of the country until the laws of King Edmund in the tenth century. These laws also dictated the payment of the church 'scot', a penny from each hearth, payable after the harvest, and the soul 'scot', due on each death. In addition, plough arms brought in a penny from each plough in the village.

The Council of Merton, in 1305, listed some of the tithes that had to be paid at the beginning of the fourteenth century. The list was formidable in its careful detail and included tithes due by law 'on the cutting and felling of trees and woods, the pasturage of the forests and the sale of the timber; the profits of the vineyards, fisheries, rivers, dovecots, and fish-stews; the fruits of trees, the offspring of animals, the grass harvest, and that of all things sown; of fruits, of warrens of wild animals, of hawking, of gardens and manses, of wool, flax and wine; of grain and of turf, where it was dug and dried; of pea-fowl, swans, and capons; of geese and ducks; of lambs, calves, and colts, of hedge cuttings, of eggs, rabbits, of bees with their honey and wax; together with the profits from mills, hunting, handicrafts of all sorts and every manner of business.'

The greedy and insensitive parson insisted on every last bit due to him: the rakings of the harvest, the acorns from the forest, the brushwood from the hedgerows. The parson who had the welfare of his people at heart lightened the burden on the poorer villagers whenever possible, often at the expense of his own pocket. The payment of tithes affected the living standards of both the people and the parson and was in turn affected by the fortunes of the village. When the harvest was good, the community prospered and so did the parson. When the harvest was bad, both suffered equally. The parson who upset the whole delicate structure was the one who used his muscle to maintain his living standards against the downward trends.

A third source of income was from fees and offerings paid by parishioners for specific jobs such as christenings, marriages and churchings of women. There were also voluntary contributions to the church. These were at first in kind and often continued to be so: mortuary fees might be paid in the form of the family's best gown or a choice cow or bullock. When money was paid as a fee, it was always the curate's hope that he might be allowed to take the service and reap the reward. This income did not generally arouse any indignation from the community, for everyone could see immediately what they were paying for.

An income could, of course, be supplemented by the odd grant for special services. The parson of Pinhoe won such a grant for his courageous efforts in the defence of his village against a Danish raiding party up the Exe estuary in AD 1001. The defenders of Pinhoe ran out of arrows, so the gallant parson volunteered to brave the Danish outposts and to run all the way to Exeter for more. He returned safely but his arrows were insufficient. The Danes burnt Pinhoe and then withdrew. Nonetheless, the parson received a reward for his valour: a grant of eight pence annually.

From this overall income, the parson had to pay his own taxes: first fruits and tenths to Rome. He also had to pay subsidies to the king, the wages of his clerk, poor relief, the expenses of the archdeacon's annual visitation and his own annual tithe dinner, diocesan taxes, a pension to his predecessor or to a church celebrity, the cost of bread, wine and chrism oil for the church, the upkeep of his parsonage and the maintenance of the chancel. The nave was the responsibility of the churchwardens and the parish. All this considered, it was hardly surprising that he was so often moved to press hard for the payment of glebe rents and tithes.

Before the Reformation, the average parson enjoyed an income of approximately £10 to £15 a year, though at least half the livings were not worth the lower figure. In cases where the rector (whether a pluralist, a monastery or a layman) had put in a vicar to take care of the parish, the great tithes (usually corn, hay and wood) went to the rector and the vicar survived on some or all of the small tithes, the insubstantial remains of the parish income (though that right to any part of the tithes could be vested by law in the vicar). The reformers of the fourteenth century were more concerned with the other side of the picture: the hardship of the peasant who paid the fees and tithes. The perfect priest, claimed Langland, should charge no money for taking special services; if he died of cold because he could not afford a coat, then that was the price of his duty; if he needed money, then he should get it from the bishop, who supposedly had lands and riches enough to pay for all the parsons in his diocese. As to tithes, Langland complained bitterly that 'The parish priest and the pardoner share the profits together, which the poor of the parish would have if these were honest.' His contemporary John Ball (one of the leaders of the 1381 Peasants' Revolt) reasonably suggested that no tithes should be paid by someone less well off than the parson himself. Wyclif proposed that each congregation should control the income of their own parson and pay him only what they thought appropriate. The protests of these honest men awakened echoes throughout the land but the sound was smothered by the Church's indifference.

Far from controlling the parson, the Church encouraged him by allowing him to issue a general curse from the pulpit against all those who sought to avoid payment of their tithes. This curse was permitted four times a year. The habit, although not the custom, evidently continued for a long time, as Thomas Moore found in the nineteenth century:

> Your priests, whate'er their gentle shamming,
> Have always had a taste for damning.

Chaucer's parson was reluctant to abuse his parishioners in this fashion. He, for one, relied on their goodwill, as a reflection of his own fair dealing:

> Full looth were hym to cursen for his tithes,
> But rather wolde he yeven, out of doute,

Unto his povre parisshens aboute
Of his offryng and eek of his substaunce.
He koude in litel thyng have suffisaunce.

For the parson who could not make a decent living out of one parish, pluralism was the only answer. Thomas Brerewode was a fine example of a successful pluralist at the time of the Reformation and built himself a splendid house at Colyton in Devon. Not only was he vicar of Colyton; he was rector of Ilfracombe, Bradninch and St Ewe; he was archdeacon of Barnstaple; he held prebends in Cornwall, Crediton and Exeter; he was chancellor of Exeter cathedral and vicar-general to Bishop Vesey; and he was a fellow of All Souls, Oxford. The dissolution of the monasteries increased Brerewode's good fortune, for he acquired a residence in Exeter cathedral close which had originally been the town house of the abbots of Buckfast. He overstepped himself eventually during an official inquiry into the irregular practices of the laity and he died in prison. In Elizabeth's Canons of 1571, no parson was allowed to hold two benefices within twenty-six miles of each other. This distance was increased to thirty miles in 1604.

Two circumstances in particular were damaging to the parson at this time. One was the increase in numbers of lay patrons, who extorted payment for the acquisition of a benefice. The other was the compulsory commutation of tithes to a fixed annual payment that made no allowance for inflation. Thus the parson started out in debt and never recovered. The parson's income in the sixteenth century was much the same as it had been in the fifteenth. In 1535, for example, out of nearly 9,000 benefices, almost half were worth less than £10 a year and of these about 3,000 were worth less than £5 and 1,000 were worth less than £2. Of the rest, about 3,600 varied in value between £10 and £26 and only 144 were worth more than £40.

Despite these low incomes, several traditional perks survived to assist the parson. One was the right to feed his geese on any common land; another was the right to receive gifts of clogs for his feet and a coarse shirt for his back; a third was the right of whittlegate, the right of the parson to use his knife at any table in the parish. There were other ways to a free meal. Lord Mounteagle left a small sum on his death in 1524 to pay for thirty priests selected to attend his funeral. News of the hand-out spread fast and eighty priests in all turned up to attend the obsequies. They did not all receive money but all had a share of the funeral feast.

The Puritans at first objected to the collection of tithes, though they soon learned the economic facts of life when they themselves became incumbents. They also found how difficult it was to collect their dues. Parishioners loyal to the Anglican incumbent refused to pay up or else raided the tithe barn and redistributed their tithes secretly to the ousted incumbent. Both Puritan and Anglican parsons at loggerheads with their parishioners might legally be stopped from crossing one man's field to obtain access to the tithes of another field beyond. Village independence could be asserted by striking a blow at the interference of the parson.

Dryden's harvest-home song summed up the feeling of triumphant defiance:

We've cheated the parson, we'll cheat him again,
For why should a blockhead have one in ten?
One in ten,
One in ten;
For why should a blockhead have one in ten,
For prating so long, like a book-learned sot,
Till pudding and dumpling burn to pot?
Burn to pot,
Burn to pot.

In self-defence, the Church published *A New Gag For An Old Goose* in 1624, which endeavoured to prove that it possessed a divine right to the tithes it received. Meanwhile the clergy themselves sought to extract every last item to eke out their living. George Herbert, on the other hand, gave one-tenth of his tithes to be distributed by his wife to the poor, but he was well-off enough to be able to afford to do so. Others were not so lucky. By the end of the seventeenth century, the parson's revenues were in general so inadequate that fathers considered it shameful for their sons to go into the Church and no respectable woman would consider marrying the average vicar. There were, of course, ways of self-help but they required the imagination and perseverance of a man like Parson Daffy of Redmile in the vale of Belvoir. Parson Daffy concocted a soothing elixir which he sold through his son's apothecary shop. The elixir claimed to relieve the symptoms of a number of common ailments and no doubt its claim was the greater because of the parson's good name.

According to Richard Gough, writing in 1701, the calculation of the tithe to be paid was almost as much of a headache as the collection of payment itself. Gough conscientiously described the assessment of tithe in the living of Myddle: 'All tythes are paide in kinde to the Rector; (viz. the tenth parte) except these customes following: . . . as for wool, lambbs, piggs, and geese, if there bee seaven, the Rector has one for tythe, and then hee must pay to the parishioner three half pence for those three that are wanting to make ten: but if there bee under seaven, then the Rector has onely an half-penny a piece for them, and does not count on till they come to ten: and soe if there bee seventeen, then the Rector has one for the ten, and one for the seaven, paying three half-pence. But if there bee above ten, and under seventeen, then the Rector has one for the ten, and a half-penny for every one that is above ten: and soe for a greater number, (although some doe count on with the Minister.)' No wonder the parson who was not nimble with numbers preferred to use an agent for the collection of his tithes!

Some degree of official help came to the parson's aid at the beginning of Queen Anne's reign. Queen Anne's Bounty was distributed to relieve the poorest of the clergy. Figures for assessing the payment of the bounty were returned in 1704–5 and were published in 1711. More than 9,000 livings were listed, all of them paying first fruits and tenths not to the Pope, as before the Reformation, but to the Crown. Of these livings, more than 5,000 were worth less than £80, more than 3,800 were worth less than £50 and more than 1,200 were worth less than £20. Subsequently, first fruits and tenths were abolished from all benefices worth less than £50 and the income from the remainder was used to augment the incomes of the poorer livings. One hundred years later, after a steady rise both in income and in the social scale, there were approximately 4,000 livings, out of a total of 10,000, worth less than £150.

At the higher end of the scale, there were many well-off curates and wealthy parsons during the eighteenth century. Parson Woodforde earned a basic £300 to £400 from his living in the 1780s, quite apart from extra income. William Sellon, who died in 1780, earned more than £1,000 a year from the various posts that he held, though these were mainly in London. John Leroo, rector of Long Melford in Sussex from 1790 to 1819, noted in his accounts how he increased the value of his living from £460 to £1,220 a year, largely through a succession of amicable agreements with his parishioners. In addition, he vastly increased the capital value of the benefice. The advowson was bought for £2,600 in 1783 and sold for £15,000 in 1819.

The Reverend Tindall Hart records in his book *Country Counting House* (1962) some transactions from the Memorandum Book of Squire Payne, rector of Barnack between 1706 and 1751, and from the Account Book of Henry Mease, rector of Alderton between 1724 and 1737 and of Swindon between 1738 and 1746. The transactions show us how both men, fellows of their respective university colleges and relatively well-off, were spending and earning their money. Mease, for example, spent liberally on food and brandy, gave generously to his servants, travelled extensively to London, Oxford, Cirencester, Bristol, Gloucester and Abergavenny, invested in pigs, beans, geese and chickens, enjoyed tobacco, snuff, bowls and card-playing and supplemented his income by becoming a clerical schoolmaster.

Payne's income, on the other hand, was supplemented by his additional posts as an archdeacon, prebendary of Liddington and agent to Lord Exeter and the Duchess of Rutland. After taxes, this brought him in a total income of between £400 and £500. His expenses were high. They included sending his boys to Eton and Cambridge and introducing his girls into county society. Like Henry Mease, he travelled widely. He spent indulgently on hemp, oysters, tea, chocolate and sugar, all of which were costly. He also gave numerous small amounts to charities and paid for such things as schooling for the children of poor families, corn for the needy, fire damage in the village, gifts to individuals and books published by the Society for the Propagation of Christian Knowledge, the SPCK. He further supplemented his income by selling malt and home-made beer to his parishioners.

Such men could afford to be generous; others could not. The rector of Hurstpierpoint in Sussex decided to go to court in 1716, 'to secure the grain that fell to the ground from the bottom of the tithe cocks'. But there were those, maybe poorer still, who were less mean. Fielding's great-hearted fictional character, Parson Adams, had only £23 a year on which to keep a wife and six children. William Jones, curate of Broxbourne, could sympathise with the parson's inability 'to make any great figure' with this sum, for he, too, had an increasing family and found his tithes hard to collect.

At Easter 1802, William Jones tried a new tack for the collection of his tithes. He issued a politely worded circular to his congregation: 'Mr Jones has the pleasure of waiting on his worthy friends and parishioners, to solicit the offerings usual at this season of the year, which constitute the chief value of the Vicarage, together with an equivalent for the tenths of gardens, etc. He hardly needs suggest to his friends that the liberality of many individuals, which cannot impoverish them, will (if it does not enrich) at least conduce to furnish him and his very numerous family with a cheerful competence, which is all that he desires, – not for his own sake only, but that, after twenty-one years' residence here already, he may be able to attend to the solemn and very important duties of his ministerial office, for the remainder of his days, with as few worldly cares and distractions as possible.'

William Jones's plea to his parishioners was not altogether unreasonable, in the light of one particular benefit that the tithe-payers enjoyed. It was a traditional custom for the parson to hold a Tithe Audit each year, so that he could receive his tithes in person at the parsonage. In return for prompt payment, he would provide a first-class dinner, during which it was the aim of the tithe-payers to eat and drink as much as they could, to get their money's worth. The moment of truth usually came after the dinner, when the parson reckoned that his guests were mollified by drink and would pay up uncomplainingly. William Cowper observed that there could still be awkwardness, even this late. Dinner is over in 'The Yearly Distress', (1779):

> At length the busy time begins.
> 'Come, neighbours, we must wag.' –
> The money chinks, down drop their chins,
> Each lugging out his bag.
>
> One talks of mildew and of frost,
> And one of storms and hail,
> And one of pigs that he has lost
> By maggots at the tail.
>
> Quoth one, 'A rarer man than you
> In pulpit none shall hear;
> But yet methinks, to tell you true,
> You sell it plaguy dear.'

Parson Woodforde usually handled his 'Tithe Frolic', as he liked to call it, with practised ease and great success. His first audit at Weston Longeville was on 3 December 1776. He noted in his diary that he gave his tithe-payers a good dinner and 'they had to drink Wine, Punch and Ale as much as they pleased, and were very happy indeed.' So was the parson. He received £236 2s od in tithes and glebe rent that evening. His guests stayed until ten at night. Twenty-three years later, in 1799, the company was still enjoying itself, despite hard times. The tithe-payers stayed until eleven at night and 'went away then highly pleased'. The parson's nephew gave them a song and Woodforde recorded with satisfaction that 'it was the pleasantest and most agreeable Tithe-Audit, I ever experienced.'

Unfortunately, there were less pleasant economic facts for Woodforde to digest at that time. The Napoleonic Wars, rising prices and public riots caused hardship for many. Even well-heeled parsons like Woodforde were constantly worried about ever increasing taxation. In 1798 he noted the payment of an extra £25 in taxes: 'Very heavy indeed are the new Taxes on the Clergy in short. How the new Taxes will go down with the People in general I know not, I hope they will not create more new Taxes after these, tho' at present are talked of.' A year later he recorded that 'I delivered this Morning my Income Tax-Paper to Js Pegg in which I have charged myself 20£ per Ann.' Five years earlier he had paid James Pegg only £7 10s 3d for taxes: that included Land Tax, House and Window Tax, Male Servant Tax, Horse Tax and Ten Per Cent Additional Tax on Assessed Tax. Several other taxes were later added to these; they included Hair-Powder and Sporting Dog Tax: both taxes hit Parson Woodforde personally.

Prices as well as taxes were rocketing upward at the turn of the century. In June 1796, Woodforde recorded: 'All kinds of Meat very high indeed at present.' In February 1800, he noted that the price of wheat was causing the poor to grumble. The price was £6 a quarter. Exactly a year later, wheat was £7 10s 0d a quarter and there was real distress among the poor. That was the figure paid for Woodforde's wheat. By the time the wheat was turned into bread, the price was exorbitant. A month earlier, he noted that a former sixpenny loaf was being sold for as much as seventeen pence.

Not surprisingly, the parson's tithes appeared to be an ever greater burden on the already impoverished people of the countryside in the nineteenth century. Speaking at the turn of the century, Sydney Smith spoke out against tithes. 'Tithes are a most atrocious way of paying the clergy,' he said. 'The custom of tithe in kind will seem incredible to our posterity; no one will believe in the ramiferous priest officiating in the cornfield.' He coined the word 'ramiferous' himself, in reference to the green bough which, until the beginning of the nineteenth century, was stuck into every tenth sheaf of corn to show that it belonged to the parson. As for the tithe barn, it was, according to Richard Jefferies' *Field and Hedgerow* (1889), a symbol of 'centuries of cold-blooded oppression'.

The Tithe Act of 1836 (which replaced the payment of tithe in kind with a rent charge on the land) brought some peace to the country but the money, if not the kind, had still to be collected from reluctant parishioners. The parson was no longer free to curse his congregation if they did not pay up, as he had done before the Reformation, but he was not above raising the point in church at an appropriate moment. Parson Parramore of Dunterton in Devon heard a voice from the back of his church shout out roughly during his sermon one Sunday, 'You'm payd to spake up, us can't yurr'ee down yurr.' Recognising the speaker, the parson seized his chance and shouted back from the pulpit, 'Yew awe me tew yurr's tithes, can ee yurr thaat?'

He could still collect his tithes at an annual tithe dinner, as the parson had done in the eighteenth century, but an increasing number of parsons employed agents to save themselves the social embarrassment and to ensure greater efficiency. Robert Hart, vicar of Takeley in Essex, was one of those who preferred the old, personal touch and loaded his table with boiled beef, vegetables and beer to lure in his tithe-payers. Unlike the parson in Cowper's poem, Hart made sure that he collected his tithes *before* the meal! He noticed that those who owed him only small sums of money were the most determined to consume their tithe's worth. The richest farmers did not deign to attend the dinner; they merely sent a cheque.

Another parson who continued to collect his tithes in person was the subject of a traditional Devonshire song. His unfortunate story suggests an eighteenth-century origin but such lively activities could still be found in isolated nineteenth-century parishes. The song is called 'The Tythe Pig':

All ye that like a bit of fun, come listen here awhile;
I'll tell you of a droll affair, will cause you all to smile,
    The parson drest in all his best,
    Cocked hat and bushy wig,

He went into a farmer's house to choose a sucking pig.
   'Good morning,' said the parson,
   'Good morning, Sir, to you;
'I've come to choose a sucking pig, the pig that is my due.'

Then went the farmer to the stye, among the piglings small,
He chose the very wee-est pig, the wee-est of them all;
     But when the parson saw the choice
     How he did stamp and roar!
He snorted loud, he shook his wig, he almost cursed and swore.
   (Chorus)

Then up and spoke the farmer, 'Since my offer you refuse,
'Pray step into the stye yourself, and you may pick and choose.'
     So to the stye, the priest did hie,
     And there without ado,
The old sow ran with open mouth, and grunting at him flew.
   (Chorus)

She caught him by the breeches black, that loudly did he cry,
'Oh help me, help me from the sow, or surely I shall die!'
     The little pigs his waistcoat tore,
     His stockings and his shoes,
The farmer said with bow and smile, 'You're welcome, Sir, to
     choose.'
   (Chorus)

'Go fetch me here a suit of clothes, a sponge and soap, I pray,
'And bring me my old greasy wig, and rub me down with hay,
     'Another time I won't be nice
     'In gathering my dues,
'Another time in sucking pigs, I will not pick and choose.
     'Good morning,' said the parson,
     'Good morning, Sir, to you;
'I will not pick a sucking pig, I'll leave the choice to you.'

All this was in good humour but there was still open resentment against the parson's tithes, particularly where they were
collected in kind by a mean man like the parson of Woodley in
Devon. The parson lived on tithes valued at £1,000 a year but

even so he insisted on the payment of every last ounce due to him. This provoked the local farmers to counter-attack with a simple ploy to deny the parson his full tenth of the milk yield. They only half-milked their cows on the days specified for tithe-collection. The parson retaliated with a lawsuit but was unable to prove that he was being cheated. To the delight of his parishioners, he himself ended up in Exeter gaol.

The parson of Woodley's meanness was matched by that of Parson Ormerod, in a story told to Francis Kilvert by his own mother: 'She mentions too a story which seems almost incredible but which she states is well known to be true. Mr Ormerod, the Rector of Presteign, who has a living of £1,000 a year but who is nevertheless always over head and ears in debt, has every Sunday two Celebrations of the Holy Communion at which he always puts upon the plate his pocket knife by way of alms, saying that he has no change. After the service he returns his knife to his pocket, but (it is stated) invariably forgets to redeem it.' It would seem from these two stories that in self-interest the parson and his parishioners were equally wily.

The value of the two livings, at £1,000 each, was high. Many parsons in the nineteenth century still had to rely on more than one living by which to make ends meet. Much to the indignation of the Evangelical movement, there were more livings without a resident incumbent at the beginning of the nineteenth century than there were livings with a parson in residence. The Pluralities Act of 1838 reduced the distance apart at which any two livings must be held from thirty miles to a mere ten miles. The distance was further reduced to four miles apart, by road, in 1885. Archbishop Temple was asked by one of his parsons for permission to hold a second small living adjoining his own. 'How far is it from your present one?' the bishop asked. 'About two miles, as the crow flies,' the parson replied. 'But you're not a crow,' said the bishop, 'and you shan't have it.'

Foiled in this attempt, the parson almost certainly sought another way to increase his income. There were orthodox and less orthodox means of doing so. Francis Kilvert followed the accepted practice of taking in a pupil. He gave board and lodging and full tutorial instruction to the thirteen-year-old Sam Cowper Coles for £80 a year in 1878. A practice that was also common but less acceptable was to increase the harvest yield of the glebe by growing crops in the churchyard. One parson is credited with growing variously turnips or wheat. The archdeacon discovered this enterprise and made a strong objection. 'I hope that you will not grow such a crop again in the churchyard,' said the archdeacon sternly. 'Of course not,' replied the parson, who understood the best farming methods. 'Next year, I shall grow barley.'

Considerable profits were made from smuggling by parsons in the nineteenth century. In the early years of the century, the church of Parson Barham in Romney Marsh was used as a hiding place for tobacco and gin. Combining virtue with profit, Parson Mordaunt opened a 'spiritless' pub in Warwickshire in 1876. Any woman who required 'medicinal' gin or brandy could always obtain it, at a price, from the medicine store kept by the parson at the rectory.

By such imaginative methods was the spirit of endeavour kept alive, a spirit that has remained very much in evidence during the twentieth century. Church and state had placed the parson where he was but had left his survival largely to individual initiative. The people, lumbered with the system, had little say in the matter and, not unnaturally, showed themselves less than eager to support the parson in a manner according either to his rights or to his liking. He could hardly be blamed for using that initiative and fighting for those rights. His duties to God and the parish could not, as he saw it, be decently performed if he did not first observe his duty to himself.

4

THE DUTIFUL PARSON

God is more dishonoured and the devil better served on the
Sunday than upon all the days of the week beside.

Sixteenth-century homily

Bishop: 'I have heard that you are drunk.'
Parson: 'I am never drunk on duty, my Lord.'
Bishop. 'When is a clergyman not on duty?'
Parson: 'True, my lord, I never thought of that.'

Eighteenth-century anecdote

The duties of the parson towards his church and his parishioners
changed little over the centuries. The cornerstones of his function
were to perform regular services in church, to observe the
sacraments, to preach on occasions and to visit the sick. The
only alteration, in accordance with the attitudes of the day, was
the emphasis on particular aspects of these duties.

Each year, the sidesmen reported to the visiting archdeacon
on the performance of their parson during the preceding twelve
months. It was reported in the fourteenth century that the
parson of Stoke Canon had behaved himself honestly and that all
spiritual affairs were in good order. The vicar of Colyton was
said to be upright but he did not visit the sick; his sermons were
short and bad and he never invited the preaching friars to instruct
his flock. The vicar of Sidbury was a good man but failed to
provide teaching on original sin. The vicar of Branscombe was
musical, preached well and visited the sick regularly. Parson
Blond was said to preach often but never clearly enough. In a
later report from Colyton, the sidesmen complained that the
vicar had leprosy but insisted on carrying on with the services, at
great risk to the congregation.

Baptisms, weddings and the churching of women after birth were duties that brought the parson into close touch with the everyday lives of his parishioners. So, too, did confession. Archbishop Walter Reynolds warned his parsons, when he wrote to them in 1322, to take great care to avoid any possibility of scandal during confession: 'Let the priest choose for himself a common place for hearing confessions, where he may be seen generally by all in the church; and do not let him hear anyone, and especially any woman, in a private place, except in great necessity and because of some infirmity of the penitent.'

Preparation for confirmation was also important; so was general instruction in religion. It was up to the parson to bring up the children of the parish in the Christian faith and to teach them in plain language the Creed, the Ten Commandments, the seven sacraments, the seven sins, the seven works of mercy and the seven principal virtues. He should also read often from the Bible, if he had one, if he could translate it and if he himself could read. None of these requirements was always certain to be fulfilled.

There were several medieval books of instruction to help the parson to an understanding of his duties. Perhaps the most popular was the *Sacred Handbook*, (c1486–96) written by John Myrc, which was widely read in the early sixteenth century. The handbook contained sensible advice to the country parson and included warnings against ostentatious dress, taverns and rich food. The parson was to strive for excellence in 'a society of unrestrained passion and unseemly violence'. Myrc added that 'an unlearned but humble priest is better than a learned but presumptuous one. . . . The priest of God, whose soul is in his hands, always knows that he is hired to celebrate every day . . . therefore he disposes himself to live soberly as to himself, justly as to the master he serves, and piously towards God.'

Throughout the Church's history, great emphasis was always laid on visiting the sick, though this injunction was not so often well observed. The best example, in the early years, of a conscientious visiting parson was Chaucer's friend from the *Canterbury Tales* (1387):

Wyd was his parisshe, and houses fer asonder,
But he ne lefte nat, for reyn ne thonder,
In siknesse nor in mescchief to visite
The ferreste in his parisshe, muche and lite,
Upon his feet, and in his hand a staff.

The church service was, of course, a prime duty and the
central event of the religious life of the parish. Before the
Reformation, there was generally Matins between six and seven
on Sunday morning, followed by High Mass between nine and
ten; after the midday meal, there was Evensong between about
two and three in the afternoon. Langland outlined the proper
observances for a typical Sunday in *Piers Plowman* (1360–99), with
the implication that not everyone complied:

And upon Sundays to cease, God's service to hear,
Both Matins and Masse, and after meat in churches
To hear their Evensong, Everyman ought.
Thus it belongeth to Lord, to learned and lewd,
Each holy day to hear Wholly the service,
Vigils and fasting days Further to know.

In other words, everyone was expected to turn up to all three
Sunday services and to any services on Church feast days. The
parson himself was supposed to say daily service as well. In early
times, it was common for villagers to attend daily Mass if they
were free. The Sanctus bell rang out to let the workers in the
fields know that the service was in progress, so that they might
bow their heads and pray for a moment. When attendance fell off,
the parson was liable to skip through the service or to abandon it
altogether. Several instructions were sent out at various times by
bishops and synods, reminding parsons of their duty in an attempt
to bring them to order.

The service was in Latin. Most of the people would not
understand but they took reassurance from the familiar rhythm
of the words. The parson stood at the far end of the chancel,
facing away from the people and wearing whatever fine vestments
he possessed. He preached in the vernacular but usually gave

only four sermons a year; hence the popularity among the congregation of the visiting preachers, who were generally considered to give good entertainment value.

The Reformation greatly affected the relationship of the parson and his people in church. The congregation was encouraged to join in the responses, now in the vernacular. Cranmer's Book of Common Prayer (1549) became the focal point of worship and the main source of instruction. Popish ritual was thrown out. Morning Prayer was generally at about nine o'clock and could last for two hours. Evening Prayer might last for an hour but included the catechising of children and servants. There were also daily services, and Holy Communion four times a year: at Christmas, Easter, Whitsun and after the harvest. The Act of Uniformity in 1559 made attendance at Sunday services compulsory. Fines of one shilling were imposed on householders for each of their family or servants who did not attend.

There were plenty of truants, despite this threat. In 1574, a homily, 'Of the Place and Time of Prayer', was appointed to be read in all churches throughout Queen Elizabeth's realm: 'The wicked boldness of those that will be counted God's people, who pass nothing at all of keeping and hallowing the Sunday . . . they must ride and journey on the Sunday; they must drive and carry on the Sunday; they must row and ferry on the Sunday; they must keep markets and fairs on the Sunday . . . they will not rest in holiness, as God commandeth; but they rest in ungodliness and filthiness, prancing in their pride, pranking and pricking, pointing and painting themselves, to be gorgeous and gay; they rest in excess and superfluity, in gluttony and drunkenness, like rats and swine; they rest in brawling and railing, in quarrelling and fighting; they rest in wantonness, in toyish talking, in filthy fleshiness; so that it doth too evidently appear that God is more dishonoured and the devil better served on the Sunday than upon all the days of the week beside.'

Perhaps the Reformation had not achieved as much as its enthusiasts would believe. Such ranting against wickedness was a far cry from the gentle admonishment given in *The Young Children's Book* of instruction, about the year 1500:

Aryse be tyme oute of thi bedde,
And blysse thi brest and thi forhede,
Then wasche thi handes and thi face,
Keme thi hede, and aske God grace
The to helpe in all thi werkes;
Thou schall spede better what so thou confes,
Then go to ye chyrche, and here a masse.

The Puritans were convinced that the Church of England had not gone nearly far enough from Rome. Their passion was to preach and they used their powers of oratory to spread the threat of hell-fire throughout the towns and countryside. They discarded every single sign of ornament and symbolism, including the marriage ring. Their services were full of extempore prayer, Bible study and congregational singing of the psalms, altogether more lively and exciting than the Anglican service. It was not surprising that the regular parson strongly resented the appearance of a Puritan minister on his doorstep, when he saw the welcome that some of his parishioners gave to the 'insolent' dissenter.

Ralph Josselin epitomised the Puritan love of preaching. Josselin was the vicar of East Colne in Essex at the height of Laud's power. His sermons would sometimes last up to three hours but this did not seem to upset his congregation, who commonly sent him gifts of fruit and other food. He was a conscientious churchman, strongly opposed to Laud's policies and an active fighter on behalf of the Parliamentarians. His attitude to his duties was uncompromising: 'I made a serious exhortation to lay aside ye jollity and vanity of ye time custome hath wedded us unto, and to keep the Sabbath better which is the Lord's day we are commanded to observe.'

The times in which Josselin lived were hard for those who tried to lead a religious life according to the will of God and the dictates of the Church, but there were many good men, beside Josselin, to remind them of their duty and to guide them. One of these was George Herbert, the poet, who left a portrait of his ideal priest in *The Country Parson, his Character and Rule of Holy Life*, which was published in 1652, nineteen years after his death. Herbert and Josselin were on opposite sides of the political fence.

The poet was a High Churchman and a supporter of Laud. He had once been a favourite of James I and had enjoyed the prospect of a highly successful career at court. All this he had given up to devote himself to a country parish and to 'ceaseless prayer and praise of holy living'. His portrait of the parson is idealistic but it provided a mark at which many could aim during the continued troubles of the seventeenth century: 'The country parson is full of all knowledge . . . avoiding all covetousness, neither being greedy to get, nor niggardly to keep, nor troubled to lose any worldly wealth. . . . His apparel plain, but reverend and clean. . . . The country parson hath a special care of his church that all things there be decent, and befitting his name by which it is called. . . . Secondly he considers and looks into the ignorance, or carelessness of his flock, and accordingly applies himself with catechizings, and lively exhortations. . . . The country parson preacheth constantly, the pulpit is his joy and his throne . . . is a lover of old customs, if they be good and harmless . . . desires to be all to his parish, and not only a pastor, but a lawyer also and a physician.'

A livelier approach is expressed by that corpulent historian Thomas Fuller, who survived the Civil War more by his wits than by his faith. 'To pray with the saints and play with the sinners,' was the advice that Fuller gave, in *The Holy State and the Profane State* (1642), to a sensible Christian minister. The reasonable parson, said Fuller, 'endeavours to get the general love and goodwill of his parish . . . otherwise he may preach his own heart out, before he preacheth anything into theirs. . . . He shall sooner get their goodwill by walking uprightly than by crouching and creeping.' It was good counsel, where the parson's life might well depend on the support of his parishioners.

There was, however, quite a lot of crouching to be done, for the parson had to feel his way carefully to ensure that in the pursuance of his duties he did not fall foul either of the law or of his archdeacon, whose regular visits were generously fed with news of the sins and omissions of the incumbent as seen through the ever watchful eyes of the sidesmen and churchwardens. Fornication, adultery and blasphemy were commonly listed among the parson's faults; so were his failures to visit the sick, to attend church, to catechise, baptise, instruct or to observe the proper church services in the appropriate attire. Failure to provide a number of properly instructed confirmation candidates ready for the bishop's rare summer visit could meet either with censure or with secret relief on the side of the bishop. On these visits, as many as 200 people might assemble from surrounding villages to be confirmed by the bishop in the neighbouring town. The crush was so great that there was not always time for the bishop to satisfy all his customers before he had to break off for lunch and prepare to move on to the next town before nightfall. Many candidates often missed their chance and had to wait until the bishop's next visit, perhaps a year later.

The unwary parson could fail in his duties quite unintentionally, by marrying a couple of whom one half was already either married or betrothed. This was a nasty trap, for it was hardly the parson's fault if he was deceived by the couple. Nonetheless, he took the blame if the deceit was discovered and could be punished heavily for the offence. Richard Gough related the sobering tale of Sarah, a servant girl in Shrewsbury, who married Robert Outram, a stranger and journeyman joiner. Sarah became pregnant, was dismissed by her employer and went with Outram to stay with their family. As soon as she had the baby, Outram took off and was never heard of again. Sarah later returned to Shrewsbury, went into service again and married a soldier, 'who stayed not long with her'. When it became obvious that she was pregnant once more, 'the Parish officer came to her to know who was the father to her child; and shee declared that shee was married to a Soldier that was gon, and that Mr Clarke, parson of Fitz, did marry them att a place called the Bull in the Barne.' The Parish officer presumably knew about her first marriage to Outram and was quick to seize on this second, clandestine marriage. Parson Clarke was cited to the local bishop and suspended for three years, 'which almost ruined him: but I hope he will take better care for the future.'

It was reputation rather than religion that more concerned the eighteenth-century parson, who managed on the whole to perform his necessary duties without overburdening himself by excess zeal. Even those duties were not always closely observed. Archbishop Herring noted in 1743 that, of 836 churches investigated, only 383 had both Matins and Evensong on Sundays; the rest had only one service on that day. He also noted the scarcity of communion services and weekday services in rural areas. The amount of wine consumed at communion, however, was markedly out of proportion to the number of celebrants.

Parson Woodforde managed only one service and a sermon on Sundays. He also held a service on Good Friday. He conducted four communions a year, baptised when necessary, instructed confirmation classes, visited the sick and supported the poor with donations. He also encouraged his congregation to join in the singing in church. Although the parson was apparently more concerned with the pleasures of country life than with church observances, he did know his duties and they were not always pleasant ones to perform.

On 28 January 1787, Parson Woodforde had to bury the five-week-old daughter of the Harrisons. It was not the first time he had had to bury a baby. 'I think that I never felt the cold more severe than when I was burying the above Infant,' he wrote in his diary. Perhaps the effect of the weather was compounded with his own sadness. Parson Smith of Lambourn in Berkshire also found that the weather increased his discomfort at funerals, so he performed the burial service from a specially built sentry box, which protected his wig.

In October 1777, Woodforde displayed the sterner side of his principles when he refused to christen a child. 'Harry Dunnell behaved very impertinent this morning to me,' he wrote, 'because I would not privately name his child for him, he having one Child before named privately by me and never had it brought to Church afterwards.' In the circumstances, the parson's refusal was perfectly reasonable but Harry Dunnell had further provocation to offer: 'He had the Impudence to tell me that he would send it to some Meeting House to be named etc. – very saucy indeed.'

Woodforde showed his impatience with the law when he

reluctantly performed a forced marriage, some time later. A pregnant woman could get a man imprisoned by accusing him of being the father. Sometimes the man might be completely innocent but was trapped into either paying the maintenance or marrying the girl. In January 1787, Woodforde recorded that he 'rode to Ringland this Morning and married one Robert Astick and Elizabeth Howlett by Licence, Mr. Carter being from home, and the Man being in Custody, the Woman being with child by him. The Man was a long time before he could be prevailed on to marry her when in the Church Yard; and at the Altar behaved very unbecoming. It is a cruel thing that any Person should be compelled by Law to marry. I recd. of the Officers for marrying them 0.10.6. It is very disagreeable to me to marry such Persons.' On another occasion, the parson received his fee of 2s 6d for publishing the banns of 'one Flood' but had to return the money at Flood's request because the young man was 'afterwards forbid by the girl'.

Parson Woodforde was not the only one to have problems when trying to marry people. Some of his colleagues, with much larger congregations, had far greater problems. Joshua Brooks was eccentric and quick-tempered, stout and small, a brilliant scholar and an innocent abroad in a confusing world. One Easter Monday, he had more couples to join together than he could cope with, so, rather than delaying things by asking who was to marry whom, he seized whoever was nearest and told the couples to 'sort yourselves when you go out'. When one bridegroom kissed another's bride, according to local custom, Brooks turned on him sharply. 'Friend,' he snapped, 'dip in thy own treacle.' He had problems with baptisms also. Once when flustered by a long list of elaborate names given by a proud father, he pronounced firmly, 'I'll have no more of these fine names; I shall christen it plain John.' It was only after the service that he was tactfully told the baby was a girl.

In many parishes, it was often necessary for a young couple to get the approval of the parson before they wed. If he did not think the marriage a suitable one, for any reason, he could refuse to read the banns. It was not so easy in those days to go off to another parish to have them read, for there were strict laws with regard to residence qualification. An apocryphal nineteenth-century anecdote tells how a country parson questioned a would-be bridegroom on his proof of residence. 'Do you sleep in the parish?' asked the parson. 'Yes, Sir,' replied the young man with beaming innocence, 'I have slept through several of your sermons.'

Francis Kilvert told a story the very awfulness of which confirms its likely truth. Once, when a colleague of his was publishing banns, 'he meant to say, "Why these two persons may not lawfully be joined together in Holy Matrimony". But what he did say was, "Why these two backsides may not lawfully be joined together in Holy Matrimony". Everyone in Church hid their faces. When he came out of Church I said, "Well you *have* done it now." "What?" said he. I told him. "God forbid," said he. "It is true," I said.'

Rustic innocence perhaps lent more charm and more confusion to the execution of the parson's duties than any other single factor. Kilvert found marvellous material with which to relieve the duller side of the curate's daily round. He went once on behalf of the vicar, Mr Venables, to visit a mad woman in her bedroom. 'I tried to bring some serious thoughts back into her mind,' and so he asked, ' "Whom do you pray to when you say your prayers?" She replied, "Mr Venables." It was the dim lingering idea of someone in authority.' The curate met with similar gentle frustration in his attempts to instruct the children in the scriptures: 'At the Scripture Lesson at the school this morning asking Eleanor Williams of Paradise, "What happened on Palm Sunday?" she replied, "Jesus Christ went up to heaven on an ass." This was the promising result of a long struggle to teach them something about the Festivals of the Church.'

Even in the performances of the services themselves, a thousand years of patient teaching and all the parson's conscientious sense of duty could be defeated simply by the isolation and unconcern of certain country villages. Kilvert repeated a story that came to him at second hand from the archdeacon of Sarum: 'The Archdeacon on a Visitation tour came to a small

Rev Benjamin Legge Symonds MA, Rector of Hoversham, Buckinghamshire, with a vamping horn for magnifying voices for singing in church, c1900 (*Buckinghamshire County Museum*)

The sexton, Fairford Church, Gloucestershire, 1916 (*Institute of Agricultural History and Museum of English Rural Life, University of Reading*)

Sunday School, Wiveliscombe, Somerset, *c1895* (*Institute of Agricultural History and Museum of English Rural Life, University of Reading*)

Well dressing, Tissington, Derbyshire, 1899 (*Birmingham City Library*)

upland parish in the diocese of Salisbury. He asked the clerk how often Holy Communion was administered in the year. The clerk stared. "What did you please to say?" he asked. "The Holy Communion," repeated the Archdeacon. "How often do you have it in the year?" The clerk still stared open-mouthed in hopeless bewilderment. At length a suspicion of the Archdeacon's meaning began to dawn faintly upon him. "Aw," he blurted out. "Aw, we do never have he. We've got no tackling." '

With 'tackling' and with sense of duty, the Church endeavoured to impose its rule on parson and parishioners alike but in country parishes the force of custom can often overwhelm authority. Kilvert heard another story that seems to symbolise the compromise between duty to the Church and deference to the people that the wise parson must come to recognise. It was the custom in one parish for the men and boys to play football on Sunday evenings. It was the duty of the parson to stop them doing so. Time and again, he would catch the ball and stab the bladder with his knife. Time and again, the men replaced the ball and went on playing. 'Well,' said the parson, 'it must go on.' And so it did. No laws or sermons could prevail.

5

THE PARSON IN THE PULPIT

There is, perhaps, no greater hardship at present inflicted on
mankind in civilised and free countries than the necessity
of listening to sermons.

Anthony Trollope

His jokes were sermons and his sermons jokes.

Lord Byron on Sydney Smith

The pulpit was a public platform exclusive to the parson, the
dream of every man of power and influence. From it, he could
assert his opinions and argue his advantage, clothed in all the
trappings of authority. He could guide, control and criticise or
comfort and instruct. He might flatter the squire or show off to
the people. He might bore them, inspire them or insult them, as
he wished. Too often, what he said was taken by the ignorant as
gospel truth. 'As I take my shoes from the shoemaker and my
coat from the tailor,' said Oliver Goldsmith (1730–74), 'so I
take my religion from the priest.'

Before the Reformation, the parson's rare sermons were not
so often vehicles for personal comment, nor in fact did they have
much to do with Christ or the Bible. What the congregation
liked was a colourful and dramatic story about a saint or martyr.
Well-known heroic and allegorical stories were passed round
from parish to parish. A collection of the most popular was made
by John Myrc and this was widely circulated among parsons at a
loss for subject matter.

During Elizabeth's reign, Archbishop Whitgift encouraged
parsons to preach not just four times a year but at least once a
month. The old allegories were replaced by stories from the
Bible but there was strict control over those who were allowed

to produce their own sermons. Many parsons were only permitted to read one of the score of approved homilies and a great number of these men gave no sermons at all but instead called in an itinerant preacher. In one survey in Essex, half of the 335 benefices were found to be held by 'ignorant and unpreaching' ministers. The Puritans referred scathingly to 'dumbe dogg' curates but the word of God as they themselves delivered it was more concerned with the punishments of hell-fire than with mercy or love.

The sermon became more and more a vehicle for the parson's own opinions and for political propaganda in the seventeenth century. Curious titles were offered to catch the interest of the public, who would flock to hear something as intriguing as 'The Church's Bowel Complaint' or 'A Pack of Cards to Win Christ' or 'The Spiritual Mustard Pot to make the Soul Sneeze with Devotion'. The poet Herrick (1591–1674) found a more forceful way to win the attention of his congregation. He is reputed to have thrown his sermon at the heads of those who were day-dreaming. His fellow poet, Andrew Marvell (1621–78), did not think much of the sermons of his day. 'An ounce of mother wit is worth a pound of clergy,' he remarked.

George Herbert declared that the proper sort of country parson 'preacheth constantly' but there were those who tired of the same old tune. One curate was accused by the Puritans of 'delivering his old notes as sermons for the past twenty years'. John Earle, Bishop of Salisbury, described another such preacher, in 1628, in his *Microcosmographie, or a Piece of the World Charac-terized*: 'The pace of his sermon is a full career, and he runs wildly over hill and dale, till the clock stop him. The labour of it is chiefly in his lungs; and the only thing he has made *in* it himself, is the faces. . . . His action is all passion and his speech inter-jections. He has an excellent faculty in bemoaning the people and spits with a very good grace. . . . He preaches but once a year, though twice on Sunday; for the stuff is still the same, only the dressing is a little altered: he has more tricks with a sermon, than a tailor with an old cloak, to turn it, and piece it, and at last quite disguise it with a new preface.'

'A sleepy congregation in a Scottish church', 1785 (*Mansell Collection*)

The Puritans, on the whole, were less concerned with the stopping of the clock. Every respectable pulpit was equipped with an hour-glass, which some of the Commonwealth preachers would happily turn two or even three times in one sermon. The congregation might watch the sands run low with keen anticipation of the end but the parson had only to stretch out his arm, without pausing. Daniel Burgess, warming to his own sermon against the evils of drink, permitted himself a wry joke when he noticed that several of his congregation were beginning to yawn. Drink was the subject and drink the appropriate pun. 'Therefore, my friends and brethren,' said he, raising his arm to the 'clock', 'we will have another glass before we go.'

The sermons of Parson Burgess were full of good matter but there were plenty of parsons reputed to preach endlessly on apparently nothing, with no other passion than the sound of their own voice and the knowledge of their hold over their trapped parishioners. 'It is a wonder to me how men can preach so little and so long,' wrote Owen Felltham, in his *Resolves Divine, Moral and Political* (1620): 'so long a time, and so little matter. . . . I love not those cart-rope speeches, which are longer than the memory of man can fathom. . . . Eloquence is a bridle, wherewith a wise man rides the monster of the world, the people.'

Another unsatisfactory reason for a long and often incomprehensible sermon was the parson's wish to parade his erudition in front of the squire and to flatter his patron. There was far too much 'high tossing and swaggering, besprinkling all their sermons with plenty of Greek and Latin', noted Dr Eachard, in his *Grounds and Occasions of the Contempt of the Clergy* (c 1698). 'This Learned way of Talking,' he went on, 'tho' for the most part, it is done meerly out of Ostentation, yet sometimes (which makes not the Case much better) it is done in Compliment and Civility to the all-wise Patron, or all-understanding Justice of the Peace, in the Parish.' A better reason for a long sermon, according to the curate of Pinner in Middlesex, was to keep the Puritans out of his church, when they tried to take it over for afternoon meetings. The curate kept preaching until six in the evening to foil the Puritan minister.

One man who did have it in his power to spike the guns of a long-winded parson was the parish clerk. A man as cunning as the clerk of Holy Trinity Church in Kingston-upon-Hull could perform his normal duties with nicely calculated planning to frustrate the sermon. 'When there is any sermon,' it was said, 'as commonly and for the most part there is every Sunday and holy day, he so consume the tyme with organes plainge and singinge and furder in settinge forwarde the clocke, that there can be no convenient tyme for the worde to be preached, and where as the preacher and minister have rebuked him for the same, he dothe not amend but rather is worse and worse.'

An over-hasty parson at the time of the Great Plague in 1665 was said to have encountered another awkward reaction to his sermon, when he was compelled to preach in several villages over a wide area. He had composed a fine sermon on the subject of the plague with which to greet one distressed parish and had then moved on quickly to another parish, as yet untroubled by the plague. It was, therefore, with some shock that the villagers heard him declaim, 'For these vices it is that God hath visited you and your families with that cruel scourge the plague which is now spreading everywhere in this town.' The mayor sprang up in great agitation. 'For God's sake, Sir,' he cried, 'where is the plague that I may take measures to prevent it spreading?' 'The plague, Sir?' said the vicar in surprise. 'I know nothing about the plague; but whether it is in the town or not, it is in my sermon.'

It was not surprising at that time that forebodings of disaster encouraged a few wild sermons on the end of the world. Parson Mason of Water Stratford in Buckinghamshire was still preaching on that subject in 1694, when he claimed that the Second Coming was imminent in his very own parish. This brought him much publicity and gave his congregation a fine excuse to go mad with drink and dancing. Parson Mason was the only one whose death was brought about by this excitement. He suffered a quinsy from thundering out his message too often in the pulpit. There seemed a sort of justice in the way in which the Second Coming claimed its own.

Others were more careful of the content of their sermons. George Herbert had earlier described the ideal substance of a good address: 'The country parson hath read the Fathers, and the schoolmen, and the later writers, or a good proportion of all, out of which he hath compiled a book and body of divinity which is the storehouse of his sermons, and which he preacheth all his life; but diversely clothed, illustrated and enlarged.' In a similar vein of reason and common sense, Archbishop Tillotson compiled a body of sermons which provided models for many country parsons in the eighteenth century. When Tillotson died in 1694, his wife was offered £2,000 for the copyright of the archbishop's sermons.

Perhaps the most popular of all seventeenth-century parsons

must have been the vicar who was said always to study the weather after announcing the text of his sermon. In summer, if the sun was shining, he would lay down his papers and recommend his congregation to go out and enjoy themselves. In winter, if the day was cold and unpleasant, he would suggest that the people return to the warmth of their own hearths. In either case, he knew quite well that a sermon had little chance of keeping their attention.

It certainly had no chance at all of keeping anyone's attention if it was as boring as that described much later by Oliver Goldsmith in his *Essays* (1765). 'The clergy are nowhere so little thought of, by the populace, as here,' he wrote, 'and though our divines are foremost with respect to abilities, yet they are found last in the effects of their ministry; the vulgar, in general, appearing no way impressed with a sense of religious duty . . . Their discourses from the pulpit are generally dry, methodical and unaffecting: delivered with the most insipid calmness; insomuch that should the peaceful preacher lift his head over the cushion, which alone he seems to address, he might discover his audience, instead of being awakened to remorse, actually sleeping over his methodical and laboured composition.'

The sermons of the Methodist and Evangelical preachers of the eighteenth century were very different. Complaining of the dullness of the average Anglican address, they accused it of becoming strangled by its own complex metaphors. Its prime aim, they said, was to flatter the squire rather than to exhort the people. John Berridge, in particular, among the new preachers, was renowned for the remarkable effect of his sermons. Members of his congregations were said to go into convulsions from which they recovered wholly purged and at peace. Berridge was the vicar of Everton in Bedfordshire and died in 1793. During his active life, he rode up to a hundred miles and preached ten or twelve sermons every week, addressing crowds of 5,000 people at a time in the open fields.

The highly emotional style of preaching adopted by John Berridge so successfully could easily become absurd in a lesser man, as the poet, George Crabbe (1754–1832), observed:

Loud grew his voice, to threat'ning swell'd his look;
Above, below, on either side he gazed.
No more he read his preachments pure and plain,
But launch'd outright, and rose and sank again.
At times he smiled in scorn, at times he wept.

In great contrast to John Berridge was the style of Laurence
Sterne, author of *Tristram Shandy* (1760–7) and pluralist parson
at one time or another of the livings of Sutton and Stillington
and the curacy of Coxwold. Clever and urbane but conscientious in his duties, Sterne became fashionable both as a
preacher and as a guest. It was said of him by Dr Johnson that he
was engaged to dinner for three months on end. Sterne's fictional
Parson Yorick was accustomed, in the preparation of his sermons,
to make notes for himself at the bottom of each sheet of paper.
These notes would remind him of the pace at which he should go:
'moderato' or 'so so' or 'adagio'. On one occasion he let creep
in a mild vanity and with great courage wrote 'Bravo'. The
accolade was scribbled in a corner of the sheet, where it would
be covered by his thumb, but modesty got the better of him
and he drew a line through it.

A bolder man than Yorick was Parson Davey of Lustleigh in
Devon, who was determined to preserve for posterity his vast
output of sermons during the 1770s. He found it too expensive
to pay a publisher to do this for him and so he bought a printing
press and, with the help of his maid, produced his mighty corpus
in twenty-six octavo volumes. He sent them proudly to the
Bishop of Exeter. A long time later, he received a curt acknow-
ledgement of his gift from the bishop's secretary. There was no
reward, no comment and no certainty that the bishop had read a
single word.

Ex-curate John Trusler proved to be a great deal better than
Parson Davey at promoting his own work when in 1769 he set out
a proposal to print 150 sermons, each at one shilling. The chief
attraction of the scheme was that the sermons were printed in
imitation handwriting, so that any idle parson could let slip a
glimpse of them to impress the parish with his own endeavour.

THE PARSON IN THE PULPIT

Trusler circulated every parish in the kingdom and received an overwhelming response. In a short time, he became a rich man. Such cheap tricks were not for Parson Woodforde. In May 1793, he bought one octavo volume of John Knox's sermons at a cost of 6s 6d. We do not know whether he delivered them verbatim or read them for inspiration.

One Shropshire vicar of the nineteenth century might have done better to opt for either Knox or Parson Davey. Instead, he piled his pulpit high with massive folio volumes to which he diligently referred whenever wishing to prove some obscure theological point far above the heads of his congregation. Bored to rebellion each tedious Sunday, the people seized their chances whenever the vicar was studying his books and slipped out of the church one by one, as if in some cleverly reversed game of grandmother's footsteps. Only the curate was left behind but eventually, one candle-lit winter's evening, he could bear it no longer. 'Sir,' he said, boldly interrupting a long quote from St Augustine, 'when you've done, perhaps you'll blow out the candles, lock the door, and put the key under the mat.' Without waiting for an answer, he too left the church.

Thomas de Quincey (1785–1859) found the same feature to criticise that John Earle had exposed in sermons two centuries earlier; namely, repetition. A curate was the culprit this time. 'He had composed a body of about 330 sermons,' wrote de Quincey, 'which thus, at the rate of two every Sunday, revolved through a cycle of three years; that period being modestly assumed as sufficient for insuring to their eloquence total oblivion. Possibly to a cynic, some shorter cycle might have seemed equal to that effect, since their topics rose but rarely above the level of prudential ethics; and the style, though scholarly, was not impressive.' Perhaps de Quincey would have preferred Parson Joseph Arkwright, whose honesty as to his limitations enabled him to preach one sermon only each year and that, no doubt, the same one every time.

Anthony Trollope was very blunt about the sermons of the day, in *Barchester Towers* (1857): 'No one but a preaching clergyman has, in these realms, the power of compelling an audience to sit silent and be tormented. No one but a preaching clergyman can revel in platitudes, truisms and untruisms, and yet receive, as his undisputed privilege, the same respectful demeanour as though words of impassioned eloquence, or persuasive logic, fell from his lips.' With nicer wit, George Eliot touched on another familiar failing, in *Scenes of Clerical Life* (1857). 'Mr Furness preached his own sermons, as any of tolerable acumen might have certified by comparing them with his poems,' she wrote; 'in both, there was an exuberance of metaphor and simile entirely original, and not in the least borrowed from any resemblance in the things compared.' Thackeray's Parson Crawley (in *Vanity Fair*, 1847–8) side-stepped the whole problem of sermons by getting his wife to write them for him.

In *Middlemarch* (1871–2), George Eliot described her own secret method of getting through a really bad sermon. The first thing to do, one of her characters explained, is to enjoy the end of the sermon, which is not difficult, because the agony is over. Then it is necessary to appreciate the middle of the sermon, because that is half-way to the end. It is eventually possible to be reconciled to the beginning of the sermon, because, having started, it must logically progress toward the middle and the end.

There was one parson whose style and approach George Eliot did appreciate. That was the Reverend Martin Cleves, also from *Scenes of Clerical Life*: 'Mr Cleves has the wonderful art of preaching sermons which the wheelwright and the blacksmith can understand; not because he talks condescending twaddle, but because he can call a spade a spade, and knows how to disencumber ideas of their word frippery.' An apocryphal story describes how one young clerical socialist firebrand imitated Parson Cleves's straightforward speaking. 'I believe in calling a spade a spade,' shouted the cleric from the pulpit one Sunday. 'And I say one no trumps,' called out the squire, startled into wakefulness.

Parson Cleves might also have enjoyed the sermons of Parson Thomas of Disserth, whose simplicity of style and naturalness of expression greatly appealed to Francis Kilvert. Parson Thomas would get up into his pulpit with no idea of what to say. After

The Christmas sermon, from Washington Irving's *Old Christmas*, 1892 (*Eileen Tweedy*)

rambling on about the weather for a while, the parson might casually direct his sermon towards the subject of Noah's Ark: 'Mr Noe, he did go on with the ark, thump, thump, thump. And the wicked fellows did come and say to him, ''Now, Mr Noe, don't go on there, thump, thump, thump, come and have a pint of ale at the Red Lion. There is capital ale at the Red Lion, Mr Noe.'' For Mr Noe was situated just as we are here, there was the Red Lion close by the ark, just round the corner. Yes indeed.

But Mr Noe he would not hearken to them, and he went on, thump, thump, thump.'

George Borrow would certainly have found such a sermon a strange contrast to the more formal, written sermon to which he was accustomed, just as in *The Romany Rye* (1857) he found a more sophisticated and eloquent extempore sermon at first greatly disturbing. 'And on this text the clergyman preached long and well,' he wrote, 'he did not read his sermon, but spoke it extempore; his doing so rather surprised and offended me at first; I was not used to such a style of preaching in a church devoted to the religion of my country. . . . Did it not savour strongly of dissent, methodism, and similar low stuff? . . . However, long before the sermon was over I forgot the offence which I had taken, and listened to the sermon with much admiration, for the eloquence and powerful reasoning with which it abounded.'

Such eloquence was not for the likes of humble curates addressing rustic congregations amid the mild distractions of warm, wet, unexciting autumn days. 'I went to Bettws in light rain and preached extempore on the Good Samaritan from the Gospel for the day,' wrote Kilvert in his diary. 'A red cow with a foolish white face came up to the window by the desk and stared in while I was preaching.'

That was in September, 1871. A few months later, he went to see old Hannah Whitney one evening and 'sat awhile with her'. She entertained him with two stories about the preaching of Parson Williams of Llanbedr Church, 'a good churchman but a very drunken man', who had a quick and quarrelsome temper. One night, apparently, the parson 'got fighting at Clyro and was badly beaten and mauled. The next Sunday he came to Llanbedr Church bruised black and blue, with his head broken and swollen nose and two black eyes. However he faced his people and in his sermon glorified himself and his prowess and gave a false account of the battle at Clyro in which he was worsted, but in which he represented himself as having proved victorious. The text was taken from Nehemiah xiii, 25. ''And I contested with them and cursed them and smote certain of them and plucked off their hair, and made them swear by God.'' ' 'Another time,' Hannah Whitney told Kilvert, the parson 'was to preach a funeral sermon for a farmer with whom he had quarrelled. He chose his text. Isaiah xiv, 9. ''Hell from beneath is moved for thee to meet thee at thy coming.'' '

Both these texts were fine examples of the parson's skill in wielding the powerful propaganda of authority and in commanding voiceless attention. So long as people were prepared to listen, with no more protest than raised eyebrows, the parson held the floor in every parish in the land and knew how to make good use of it, even to reach the dead.

6

PARSONS, CLERKS AND CHURCHES

> The enormous weight of ecclesiastical bricks and mortar that cumbers the land.
>
> *Richard Jefferies*

> The country parson hath a special care of his church, that all things there be decent and befitting his name by which it is called.
>
> *George Herbert*

The church in which the parson preached as if he was its lord was not intended as a place that he could call his own. It was the centre of medieval village life. The people contributed both in effort and expense to its construction and maintenance and the churchwardens existed as their representatives to ensure that the parson performed his duties in a satisfactory manner. The pulpit was a platform not only for the occasional sermon but for much more regular parish announcements and official proclamations. The wooden Saxon church, with its stone tower, its rushes to cover the floor, its decorative paintings on the walls, was both a meeting place where people might gather to gossip and a solid symbol of their protection against the terrors and mysteries of an uncertain world.

Property and land were left by many villagers, as well as by the lord, to provide revenue for the church and each parish vied with its neighbour as to the richness of the ornaments given to embellish the house where priest and people met to praise their God. The money for expensive items, like re-roofing or a new tower or bell, was raised by organised feasts and games, known as Church Ales, to which villagers from neighbouring parishes were invited. He who spent most at the feast was considered the most godly. The substance and the treasures of the church were the essential village birthright and all were equally determined to preserve them.

The churchwardens were the guardians of the church's treasures as well as watchkeepers on the parson. They were in existence by the thirteenth century and in time were being chosen annually from among the villagers. The clerk, a layman like the churchwardens, was an even more important member of the church 'staff'. By the thirteenth century, he was usually appointed by the parson but in some cases there was a conflict between the choice of the parson and the choice of the people. On one such occasion, the people's choice seized the book of the epistle from the hands of the parson's choice in the middle of the service and 'hurled him violently to the ground, drawing blood'.

The reading of the epistle and the lesson were only two of the clerk's duties. He had also to make or lead the responses and to ring the bell for services. He walked before the parson down the village street, bearing a sprinkler of holy water, and he led the way with candle and bell whenever the parson went to visit the sick. He also kept the school in many villages. He could, according to his abilities and his relations with the parson, be a great support or a considerable thorn in the flesh.

One of his regular duties was to keep order in church among the congregation. This meant controlling the general background chatter and sorting out the interminable arguments about seating arrangements. Long before the Reformation, the question of private pews aroused much controversy. 'We have heard that many quarrels have arisen against members of the same parish,' wrote Bishop Quevil of Exeter in 1287, 'two or three of whom have laid claim to one seat. For the future, no one is to claim any sitting in the church as his own, with the exception of noble people and the patrons of churches. Whoever first comes to church to pray, let him take what place he wishes in which to pray.' It was a forlorn hope that such an injunction could bring peace. Strife over pews was a permanent theme of parish life well into the twentieth century.

The changes at the Reformation in the churches themselves were equal to the changes in the form of service. All the paraphernalia of popery were cast out. All the fine ornaments for which the people had worked so hard were discarded. All the glitter of which they were so proud was torn down. Stained glass and stone altars, statues and shrines, candlesticks and rich copes, gilded crosses and decorated altar cloths, were stripped from their places. The paintings on the walls of familiar religious scenes, which had served for generations both to delight and to instruct the illiterate, were whitewashed over. The Lord's Prayer and a few scriptural texts were written up instead. A plain wooden table was put up closer to the nave to replace the 'heathen' altar at the far end of the chancel.

The church remained a gathering place, for there was no other. Communal goods were often stored in the nave, which might at times look more like a village hall or a market place than a house of God, but this did not usually cause offence, for only the chancel was considered sacred. Market stalls were also set up in the churchyard and might remain there during the service, luring people out who crept back surreptitiously to discuss their purchase with their neighbour in the pew. It was the common burden of the parson and the clerk to have to cope with such unruly, nattering congregations, with their drunkenness in church, their churchyard games and innumerable hounds running to and fro. The Archbishop of York instructed the clergy in 1552 to ensure 'that vergers do attend divine service for the expulsion of beggars, other light persons and dogs forth of the church.'

Where churches were still kept in reasonable condition by their congregations, money was raised in the traditional ways, as it continued to be until the Puritans put a stop to all festivities during the Commonwealth. Church Ales were held in Elizabethan and early Stuart times, just as they had been before the Reformation, to provide for repairs and maintenance. There were also Bridal Ales, Clerk Ales and Bid Ales to raise money for a wedding, for the support of the clerk or for the poor. Morris dancers, May games, Hocktide celebrations and Christmas mummers' plays brought in extra cash. Rates and rents also helped to pay for the costs of the church. Pew rents were paid despite injunctions

'A Journeyman Parson with a Bare Existence', and 'A Master Parson with a Good Living', after Dighton, 1762 (*British Museum*)

The country parson in the twentieth century: at a christening in 1958 in the hopfields of Kent (*Topham*), and in informal mood after a christening service at Clovelly, Devon, in 1982 (*James Ravilious, Beaford Archive*)

against private pews. Church lands were rented by smallholders and peasants as well as by the bigger farmers. Rates were charged to everyone who owned land in the parish. It was one of the duties of the churchwardens to pursue defaulters. Churchwardens became increasingly important during Elizabethan times and did not have an easy task. Not only did they have to keep an eye on the parson, on behalf of the people, but they also had to act with the parson and the constable to keep an eye on the people, to pursue vagabonds and rogues, to relieve the poor and to maintain many of the communal services of the parish, such as roads and stocks and ponds. If they were not elected by joint consent, one would be chosen by the parson and the other by the parishioners. Most responsible members of the community took their turn as churchwardens, though it was not often a popular job, but there was at least one reward. An audit dinner was held at the end of their year of office, when they gave an account of what they had achieved. The dinner was commonly held in the church, despite repeated injunctions to stop this practice.

Eating and drinking in church was an ancient tradition that continued wherever the community had nowhere else in the village to meet. In 1544, Margaret Atkinson directed in her will that a feast should be held in the church when she died; she provided for bread, ale, bacon, rabbit and mutton for all the parish. In 1623, the vicar of Storrington in Sussex was told by his parishioners that it was their right and practice to have bread and cheese and a barrel of beer in the church after evening prayers. In 1692, the vicar of Codrington in Gloucestershire was surprised, on entering his new parish, to find people playing cards on the communion table and smoking and drinking with their hats on in the sanctuary when they met to choose their churchwardens. The parish clerk informed him that this was a tradition going back at least sixty years.

Many an Anglican parson was given a hard time by churchwardens with a Puritan bias. After 1641, it was the churchwardens who had the job of removing the communion rails, levelling the chancel and taking down the crucifixes and candles on behalf of the Puritans. But it was the clerk who, increasingly, seemed to be a source of vexation and minor irritation to the seventeenth-century parson. Somehow, the parish clerk had become the butt of every joke and complaint. Thomas Milbourne, clerk of Eastham, was criticised for singing the psalms in church 'with such a jesticulous tone and altisonant voice, viz: speaking like a gelded pig, which doth not only interrupt the other voices, but is altogether dissonant and disagreeing unto any musical harmony, and he hath been requested by the minister to leave it, but he doth obstinately insist and continue therein.' The clerk of Buxted in Sussex was accused of producing a melody which 'warbled forth as if he had been thumped on the back with a stone'.

In the parish of Myddle, Richard Gough was quite severe about one clerk. Thomas Highway was 'a person alltogeather unfitt for such imployment. Hee can read but little; hee can sing but one tune of the psalmes. Hee can scarse write his owne name, or read any written hand.' Another clerk, Will Hunt, was an improvement, except for his handwriting: 'A person very fitt for the place, as to his reading and singing with a clear and audible voice,' wrote Gough, 'but for his writeing I can say nothing. Hee commonly kept a petty schoole in Myddle.' A 'petty' school was the contemporary name for a primary school.

The inadequacies of his clerk no doubt greatly affected the parson's daily peace of mind and distracted him from his religious duties and from what should have been his concern for the fabric and maintenance of the church itself. George Herbert had earlier advised the country parson to take great care to keep his church decent. 'Therefore,' wrote Herbert, 'first he takes order, that all things be in good repair; as walls plastered, windows glazed, floors paved, seats whole, firm and uniform, especially that the pulpit, and desk, and communion table, and font, be as they ought, for those great duties that are performed in them. Secondly that the Church be swept, kept clean, without dust or cobwebs.'

Herbert's words had little effect. Fifty years later, in Gough's time (1635–c1723), Bishop Secker found that some churches 'have scarce been kept in necessary repair, and others by no means duly cleared from annoyances, which must gradually bring them to decay: water undermining and rotting the foundations, earth heaped up against the outside, weeds and shrubs growing upon them . . . too frequently the floors are meanly paved, or the walls dirty and patched, or the windows ill-glazed, or it may be in part stopped up . . . or they are damp, offensive and unwholesome.'

Dr George Horne, later Bishop of Norwich, was just as critical when he went to visit a country church. 'The churchyard itself was low and wet,' he wrote, 'with a broken gate the entrance, and a few small wooden tombs and an old yew tree the only ornaments. The inside of the church answered the outside; the walls were green with damp; a few broken benches; with pieces of mats, dirty and very ragged; the stairs to the pulpit half worn away; the communion table stood upon three legs, the rails worm-eaten and half gone.'

Some elements of this decay were the continuing after-effects of the Civil War but more than half-way through the eighteenth century the poet Cowper still found many of the country churches in a sad state of disrepair. 'The ruinous condition of some of the churches gave me great offence,' he wrote in a letter, 'and I could not help wishing that the honest vicar, instead of indulging his genius for improvements, by enclosing his gooseberry bush within a Chinese rail, and converting half an acre of his glebe-land into a bowling green, would have applied part of his income to the more laudable purpose of sheltering his parishioners from the weather, during their attendance on divine service. It is no uncommon thing to see the parsonage house well thatched, and in exceeding good repair, while the church perhaps has scarce any other roof than the ivy that grows over it. The noise of owls, bats, and magpies makes the principal part of the church music in many of these ancient edifices; and the walls, like a large map, seem to be portioned out into capes, seas and promontories, by the various colours by which the damps have stained them.'

In other parishes, Cowper discovered that the squire himself had taken care of the building but had left the parson to his own devices. 'I have observed,' he noted of several places, 'that nothing unseemly or ruinous is to be found except in the clergyman and the appendages of his person . . . with a surplice as dirty as a farmer's frock.'

The music that Cowper heard from the owls, the bats and the magpies should have risen from a joyous congregation, though the parson might often wish that it did not. Church singing could be his pride or his despair. In the traditional parish, the congregation still left all the singing to the clerk and parson but in many churches the people joined in. There was little point in handing out service books and psalms to illiterate parishioners in rustic villages and they could not be expected to know the psalms by heart, so the custom was for the clerk to read or sing one line of the psalm at a time, which the congregation would then repeat, before the clerk read out the next line. The singing was accompanied by the village orchestra, which occupied the gallery and played on fiddles, flutes, bassoons and clarionets or similar instruments. If there was no orchestra, the clerk would play a pitch-pipe or a barrel organ.

Hymns were greatly encouraged by the Methodists but were in evidence long before the Wesley brothers. Nahum Tate's 'While Shepherds Watched their Flocks by Night' achieved huge popularity very early in the eighteenth century, though Tate himself died in penury. Augustus Toplady wrote 'Rock of Ages' in the 1760s while a curate at Blagdon in the diocese of Bath and Wells. In 1779, the Reverend John Newton, once a slave-trafficker and subsequently curate at Olney in Buckinghamshire, published the famous 'Olney Hymns'. The collection included 'How Sweet the Name of Jesus Sounds' and 'Glorious Things of Thee are Spoken'. There were contributions from Newton's close neighbour, William Cowper.

Unfortunately, the joyfulness of these musical delights was still marred by the performance of the clerk, which had clearly not improved since the previous century. 'If there is a man in the parish who reads and sings worse than anybody else,' sighed William Jones, 'it is used to make him church clerk.' Many clerks, however, so prided themselves on their voices that they refused to let the congregation join the singing but insisted on their right, in the absence of a choir, to perform a duet with the parson. Even then, the clerk was known to forge ahead or lag behind according to his whim, so that the two men were rarely in step and continually interrupted each other. One exasperated parson finally snapped: 'Sir, either you or I must quit.'

In the event of such an ultimatum, it could well be the parson who came off worst. 'It is a difficult matter to decide which is looked upon as the greatest man in a country church, the parson or his clerk,' wrote Cowper. 'The latter is most certainly held in higher veneration, where the former happens to be only a poor curate, who rides every Sabbath from village to village, and mounts and dismounts at the church door. The clerk's office is not only to tag the prayers with an Amen, or usher in the sermon with a stave; but he is also the universal father to give away the brides, and the standing godfather to all the newborn bantlings.' The poet summed up the situation in a deft couplet:

> There goes the parson, oh! illustrious spark,
> And there, scarce less illustrious, goes the clerk.

The duties of this great man also included the recording of births, the keeping of the church accounts, the washing of surplices and the waking of those who slumbered during service. The so-called 'sluggard-waker' used a long staff with a heavy knob attached, with which to rap the dozing men and beat the mischievous children. He also had a fox's brush, for politely stirring the sleeping females. The squire of Kinvere in Staffordshire offered Thomas, the clerk, five shillings to wake any elder or farmer who slept, however rich or important the man might be. Thomas did as he was told and brought his staff down on the squire's own head. He then held out his hand for the five-shilling reward.

Not all clerks were mischievous or troublesome, as the epitaph to Michael Turner in Warham churchyard at Horsham, Sussex, aptly demonstrates:

His duty done, beneath this stone
   Old Michael lies at rest,
His rustic rig, his song, his jig
   Were ever of the best.

With nodding head, the choir he led
   That none should start too soon;
The second too, he sang full true,
   His viol played the tune.

And when at last his age had passed
   One hundred – less eleven,
With faithful cling to fiddle string,
   He sang himself to heaven.

Nor was it only the clerk who could disrupt the service: the congregation itself could be as sore a trial to a sensitive parson as ever it had been in earlier centuries. Cowper noted the number of congregations 'who scream themselves hoarse in making the responses'; old women 'who fumble over their tattered testaments till they have found the text'; children who make 'posies in summer time and crack nuts in autumn'; squires who by their sudden waking signal the sermon to stop.

Despite the ruined state of many of the churches Cowper saw, there were also many new ones built in the eighteenth century but they were not always attractive nor did they necessarily improve the standards of worship. Inside, they were dominated by the vast three-decker pulpit, which often blocked out the sanctuary from the sight of a good proportion of the congregation. One purpose of its height was to enable the parson to overlook the high box pews, which were rather like cattle stalls, wherein village 'society' snuggled comfortably, out of the draught and fortified by the occasional nip of brandy or glass of sherry. The squire's box might boast a fireplace, an armchair, a sofa and a table. His party would talk among themselves or read the papers and write letters. Occasionally, the squire would listen out to satisfy himself that the parson's sermon was suitably deferential. The poor of the parish sat well at the back of the nave and in the side aisles, where they could probably see little of what was going on. Galleries were built in the more popular churches and from these the people could see much better. In the previous century, the anti-Laudian preacher Richard Baxter of Kidderminster had built five extra galleries to provide for the swelling congregation in his own church.

A few courageous parsons took matters into their own hands and disciplined their congregations with undisguised firmness. Such a man was Parson Grimshaw of Haworth, a fiery old prophet, whose custom it was to leave his church during the singing of the 119th Psalm and to drive the drinkers at a whip's end out of the village inn and back to the church in time for his sermon. The churchwardens of Roborough in Devon complained of similar high-handedness by their curate, Samuel May, whom they accused of throwing people out of church as well as forcing them in. The curate defended his actions by stating that the victims of eviction were rowdies who disturbed the rest of the congregation and disrupted the service. The case against him was dropped. Parson Froude of Knowstone took the toughest line of all: it was said that he fired the hay-ricks of anyone who did not come to church.

Some parsons might get their people into church without much trouble but then found that they encountered powerful distractions. The parish of Portlemouth overlooked the river estuary at Kingsbridge in Devon and the parson could look out to the sea from his pulpit when the doors of the church were left open. This gave him an advantage over his congregation, who faced toward the altar, but it placed him farthest from the door if he wanted to leave quickly. It so happened that in the nineteenth century the parish enjoyed great profit from ships that were wrecked along the coast. The rule was, first come, first served. There was a storm one Sunday, the doors of the church were left open and from his vantage point the parson could see a ship being wrecked on the bar. He said nothing but descended from his pulpit and walked down the nave toward the door, as if to conduct a baptism at the font. Only when he was certain of a head start on his congregation did he turn to announce, 'My brethren,

'On reaching the church-porch, we found the parson rebuking the gray-headed sexton for having used mistletoe.'

Parson and sexton, from Washington Irving's *Old Christmas*, 1892 (*Eileen Tweedy*)

there is a wreck on the bar but let us all start fair.' With that, he raced ahead and reached the wreck first.

In the nineteenth century, there seemed to be many more incidents of parsons and clerks trying to keep parishioners away from church, to save themselves some bother. John Bythesea, rector of Bagendon in Gloucestershire, would send his clerk to the church with a bag of sixpences to be distributed among would-be worshippers to induce them to go home. The rector of Perivale, near Ealing, offered an even better bribe. His butler waited at the church door to invite the congregation for a glass of ale at the rectory in preference to Matins. Quite often, there was a misunderstanding between the parson and his clerk, or a deliberate battle about use of the church. One vicar decided to keep his church open for private prayer and placed an invitation in the porch for anyone who cared to enter. Some time later, he asked his clerk if there had been much response to the invitation. The clerk was reassuring. 'Yes, Sir,' he said, 'and I soon turns 'em out.'

In the early part of the century, when there were still a great many non-resident parsons, even a conscientious man was hard-pressed to get round all his parishes every Sunday. It was said to be a familiar sight to watch the 'black rooks' riding urgently from church to church to attend their various congregations. Too many times, they were delayed and congregations would wait in vain for the service to begin. Many villagers did not turn up for church until they heard the bell rung by the clerk as a signal that from his look-out on the tower he had seen the priest approaching.

Other parsons made no effort to go near their churches. A Cornish vicar of the 1870s was asked by his bishop to attend the services given in his own parish. The man declined and pointed out that the parish was adequately served by the neighbouring incumbent, whom he could persuade to ride over at any time. The vicar himself was more usually to be found strolling in his rectory garden in a flowered dressing-gown, smoking a hookah and chatting with his parishioners over the garden gate as they filed out of Sunday service. One church had for so long been abandoned by its parson that when a visiting preacher at last came to take a service and was about to enter the pulpit, he was warned by the clerk, 'Ye moan't go in theer, Sir, our old turkey hen's a sitting.' Occasionally there was good reason for closing down an isolated, inaccessible church during the winter, as Bishop Jackson was told when he tried to admonish the vicar of such a parish. 'Satan himself, my Lord,' replied the vicar, 'couldn't get there in the winter and I am always before him in the spring.'

At the beginning of the nineteenth century many churches were in a state of decay. 'The altar was represented by a small rickety deal table,' wrote Dean Hole of his childhood church, 'with a scanty covering and faded and patched green baize, on which were placed the overcoat, hat and riding whip of the officiating minister. . . . The font was filled with coffin ropes, tinder boxes, and brimstone matches, candle ends, etc. It was never used for baptism. Sparrows twittered and bats floated beneath the rotten timbers thereof, while beetles and moths and all manner of flies found happy homes below. The damp walls represented in fresco "a green and yellow melancholy", which had a depressing influence upon the spirit, and the darkest and most dismal building of the parish was that called the house of God.'

Parson Atkinson of Danby in Cleveland found the altar of his church covered in rags and spread thickly with stale crumbs. 'It seemed impossible not to crave some explanation of this,' he wrote 'and the answer to my enquiry was as nearly as possible in the following terms: "Why, it is the Sunday School teachers. They must get their meat somewhere and they gets it here." ' Those teachers were behaving in the fine tradition of the original Saxon community, who had used their church for mutual benefit and as a centre of social activity. Such traditions did not suit the nineteenth century.

After the reforms of the 1830s, there was a great upsurge of zeal among parsons and their parishioners. Many churches were restored and redecorated, with Victorian enthusiasm. The ponderous three-decker pulpits were thrown out and so were the great box pews. Some pew-holders resisted the collapse of their privileged protection. Dr Cooper of Woodmancote pulled down the pew belonging to the West family and was taken to court for his effrontery. Parson Sweet of Colkirk in Norfolk removed the private pew of a former incumbent, in which had been installed the parson's own convenience.

Richard Jefferies remained dissatisfied by these reforms. In *Field and Hedgerow* (1889), he complained bitterly that the very structure of the church was a burden on the land. Religion preyed on the superstitions of the poor, he wrote, and persuaded them to maintain churches, chapels and ministers when they could not afford for themselves the basic necessities of drainage, hospitals or education. The very sight of a church was anathema to him. 'I wish the trees, the elms, would grow tall enough and thick enough to hide the steeples and towers which stand up so stiff and stark, and bare and cold,' he wrote. 'At intervals came the distant chimes of three distinct village churches – ding, dong, dong, ding; pango, frango, jango – very much jango – bang, clatter, clash – a human vibration and dreadful stir. The country world was up in arms . . . en route to its various creeds, some to one bell, some to another, some to ding dong, and some to dong ding.' His sentiments caught a faint echo from Robert Burns:

> A fig for those by law protected!
> Liberty's a glorious feast!
> Courts for cowards were erected,
> Churches built to please the priest.

A succession of new hymns appeared during the century and many became popular favourites. In 1811, James Edmeston wrote 'Lead Us Heavenly Father, Lead Us' and in the same year Parson Heber of Hodnet in Shropshire, who later became a bishop, wrote 'Brightest and Best of the Sons of the Morning'. Francis Lyte, vicar of All Saints, Brixham, celebrated the sunset from Berry Head in 'Abide With Me', written in 1845. The reverend and knighted Parson Baker produced 'The King of Love My Shepherd Is' and followed it up with *Hymns Ancient and*

The interior of Deepdale Church, Derbyshire, from T. C. Bolton's *Abbeys and Churches*, 1890 (*Eileen Tweedy*)

Modern in 1861. This classic and enduring collection greatly shocked a number of congregations by the originality of some of its compositions but they soon learnt to enjoy them. Ten years later, the Reverend John Ellerton published *Church Hymns*, among which was one of his own compositions: 'The Day Thou Gavest, Lord, Is Ended'.

The hymns themselves were complemented by a revolution in the production of church music. Village orchestras were replaced by barrel organs, pipe organs and harmoniums. The parson who had a barrel organ could no longer be held to ransom by an orchestra which threatened a strike or lock-out; no more need he be worried by the disappearance of the choir to wet their throats at the pub before the anthem; he could forget the subterfuges of the pipe-playing clerk. He had at last a machine that would obey him instantly. It could, of course, go wrong. There had been barrel organs for years but now they came with a selection of one or two dozen tunes, some secular, some sacred. The secular tunes were often rousing drinking songs, for the pleasure of parishioners outside church services, but the music could sometimes, by mistake or otherwise, be changed. It was not unknown for the barrel organ to move on to a stirring ditty when the solemn hymn had died away.

The introduction of a new harmonium was another exciting event. On 29 October 1874, Francis Kilvert recorded in his diary: 'This morning was an epoch in the history of Langley Church and the first sound of an instrument within the old walls an event and sensation not soon to be forgotten.' In this case, there was a story behind the new instrument and possible trouble ahead, as Kilvert explained: 'How this innovation, necessary though it has become, will be received by the Squire no one can tell. He has forced us to do it himself and opened the way for the change by dismissing George Jeffries, the chief singer, from his post of leader of the Church singing, but we expect some violence of language at least.' The day of reckoning came on Sunday, Allhallowmas Day: 'All has gone off well,' wrote Kilvert with relief. 'Fanny played the harmonium nicely and the singing was capital. The congregation were delighted and some of them could hardly believe their ears and the Squire said nothing for or against, but he came to Church twice.' Surely, that was the seal of approval!

If Langley's new harmonium stimulated in the congregation, the curate and the squire a sense of shared pleasure, then it performed a great service, in line with the true function of the parson, to bring together all members of the community in worship. If parson and curate had done their duty well and helped to bring about that sense of sharing, then they had reason to be proud. There was 'one memorable day when Francis Kilvert enjoyed a mug or two of Herefordshire cider in the home of a friendly Welsh vicar. The man fetched down the keys to his rural parish church and said, with a twinkle in his eye, 'I am bishop here. Come and see the Cathedral.' His pride was the pride of his parishioners as well.

7
THE PARSON AND THE PEOPLE

The village wept, the hamlets round
Crowded the consecrated ground;
And waited there to see the end
Of Pastor, Teacher, Father, Friend.

William Combe

Dull though important, peevish tho' devout,
With wit disgusting, and despised without,
Saints in design, in execution men,
Peace in their looks and vengeance in their pen.

George Crabbe

The parson had no real place in the parish unless he won the
support and confidence of the community. Contact outside the
church was no less important than that within and before he
attempted to steer his congregation toward the distant goal of life
hereafter he had first to help them through the complications of
earthly existence. 'I have always believed that a house-going
parson makes a church-going people,' wrote Edward Boys
Ellman in the nineteenth century, 'and so I tried to influence my
parishioners by showing interest in them and their families, to
lead them by love.'

Another nineteenth-century parson, the Reverend Baring-
Gould, picked out a similar theme from an inscription on a
tombstone that he found in his own parish of Lew Trenchard in
Devon. The name of the long-dead priest had been worn away by
time and the weather but his example survived:

The Psalmist's man of yeeres hee lived a score,
Tended his flocks allone, theire offspring did restore

> By water into life of grace; at font and grave,
> He served God devout: and strived men's soules to save.
> He fedd the poore, lov'd all, and did by Patten showe,
> As pastor to his flocke, ye way they shoulde go.

'Example' was also the key virtue attributed by Chaucer to his Canterbury parson, who understood only too well that hard work must come before hard prayer:

> This noble ensample to his sheep he yaf,
> That first he wroghte, and afterward he taughte . . .
> To drawen folk to hevene by fairnesse,
> By good ensample, this was his bysynesse.

Such men were blessed with common sense but they also needed courage, for their involvement with the practical affairs of parish life made them the champions of the people against the pressures and injustice of authority, whether it was king or lord, abbot or squire. The parson experienced the problems of the villagers at first hand and it fell to him to become the leader for social reform, a duty that at times conflicted with his own conservative instinct for the survival of the establishment.

John Ball was a country parson in the fourteenth century, who for twenty years preached around the villages from the steps of parish churches, exhorting the people to cast off their serfdom. He was excommunicated for speaking out against the pope and the bishops, imprisoned, freed by the rebels whom he had encouraged, and eventually captured, hung, drawn and quartered. He preached his final sermon before the peasant army at Blackheath in 1381, taking as his text the famous lines:

> When Adam delved and Eve span,
> Who was then the Gentleman?

Chaucer's parson did not meddle in such weighty political issues but in his own way knew how to bring down both gentleman and peasant to the same level before the eyes of God and all of his parishioners:

But it were any persone obstinat,
What so he were, of heigh or lough estat,
Hym wolde he snybben sharply for the nonys.

The parson's contact with the people was not by any means all solemn. There were many festivals and celebrations of ancient customs that bound the people and the church into a single community. The parson provided a Christian context for the pagan energies of his parishioners. Woven into the pattern of the year, there were, beside the main church festivals, a curious mixture of traditions, at the same time rich in symbolism and yet joyfully frivolous. There was Rogation and the blessing of the crops; there was Plough Monday, when the ploughs were decked with ribbons; there were the topsy-turvy days of the Boy Bishop's rule; the fat goose killed at Harvest Home; the rush-bearing on St Anne's Day; the pancakes and pace eggs and seed cakes and thrashing the fat hen on Shrove Tuesday. These were only a few of the highlights of parish life and at the centre of each one was the parson, one among the many revellers, yet set apart by his role, their guide and their defender.

There were times, of course, when the parson so far forgot his role as to appear indistinguishable both in dress and manner from his parishioners. Lapses of this kind were strongly criticised by John Stratford, Archbishop of Canterbury, in 1342: 'Parsons scorn to wear the tonsure, which is the crown of the Kingdom of Heaven and of perfection, and distinguish themselves by hair spreading to the shoulders in an effeminate manner, and walk about clad in a military rather than a clerical dress, with an outer habit very short and tight-fitting, but excessively wide, with long sleeves which do not touch the elbow; their hair curled and perfumed, their hoods with lappets of wonderful length; with long beards, rings on their fingers, and girded belts with precious stones of wonderful size, their purses enamelled and gilt with various devices and knives openly hanging at them like swords, their boots red and green peaked and cut in many ways; with housings to their saddles, and horns hanging from their necks; their capes and cloaks so furred, in rash disregard of the

Canons, that there appears little or no distinction between clergymen and laymen.'

No parson could get away with this sort of behaviour after the Reformation, particularly when, during Elizabeth's reign, he became a minor official of the state and held real authority over the coming and going of his parishioners. He had to be seen to set a good example. Men like Parson Gilpin of Houghton-le-Spring kept a generous eye on the poor, Gilpin retaining twenty-four poor scholars in his own house; William Harrison of Radwinter left a large sum of money to the needy in his parish; John Becke, rector of Kettlethorpe in Lincolnshire, left a rather smaller sum but it was nonetheless generous. He also left this epitaph in 1597:

> I am a Becke, or river as you know,
> And wat'red here ye church, ye schole, ye pore,
> While God did make my springes for to flow;
> But now my fountain stopt, it runs no more;
> From Church and schole mi liyfe ys now bereft,
> But to ye pore four poundes I yearly left.

The parson's official responsibility for the behaviour of his parishioners continued into the seventeenth century. Permission was required from the parson by any labourer wishing to leave the parish and there was a strict residence qualification for newcomers, as Richard Gough noted in Myddle: 'Note, that at this time 40 dayes' continuance as an housekeeper, servant or sojourner without disturbance did create a settlement in any parish. Note alsoe that if the Parish officers did require any person to avoid out of the Parish or to finde suretyes, this was not accompted a disturbance.' It was the parson's duty to make sure that the people ate fish on Friday and observed their public penances. He had also to ensure that the law relating to Sunday sports was made clear and obeyed. James I forbade bear-baiting, 'common plays' and 'unlawful exercises' but in his Declaration of Sports, in 1618, much to the fury of the Puritans, he did permit 'any lawful recreation, such as dancing, either men or women, archery for men, leaping, vaulting or any such harmless recreation', as well as 'May-games, Whitsun Ales, and Morris dances, and the setting up of May-poles and other sports therewith used, so as the same be had in due and convenient time, without impediment or neglect of Divine Service'.

His son, Charles, reaffirmed the survival of Whitsun Ales, Morris dances and May-poles in the teeth of Puritan opposition and George Herbert wisely pointed out the vital link that the old customs forged between parson and people: 'The country parson is a lover of old customs, if they be good and harmless,' he wrote. 'Particularly he loves procession, and maintains it, because there are contained therein four manifest advantages: first, a blessing of God for the fruits of the field; secondly, justice in the preservation of bounds; thirdly, charity in loving walking and neighbourly accompanying one another with reconciling of differences at that time, if there be any; fourthly, mercy, in relieving the poor by a liberal distribution and largess, which at that time is or ought to be used.'

For his part, the poet–parson Robert Herrick openly admitted that he loved the village festivals. His traditional views, in defiance of the Puritans, forced him to leave his parish of Dean Prior in Devon during the Commonwealth. He listed the most popular celebrations in one of his poems:

> For sports, for Pageantrie, and Playes,
> Thou hast thy Eves, and Holydayes . . .
> Thy Wakes, thy Quintels, here thou hast,
> Thy May-poles too with Garlands grac't:
> Thy Morris-dance; thy Whitsun-ale;
> Thy Sheering-feast, which never faile.
> Thy Harvest-home; thy Wassaile bowle,
> That's tost up after Fox i' th' Hole;
> Thy Mummeries: thy Twelfe-tide Kings
> And Queenes: thy Christmas revellings.

More than ever, in troubled times, the people needed their parson's love and guidance and he, in turn, relied on their support. This mutual relationship was apparent in the tales of ousted parsons receiving surreptitious aid from sympathetic con-

gregations. Thomas Fuller counselled all ministers to win the love
and goodwill of their parishioners before they tried to teach them
anything.

More than a hundred years later, in 1770, Oliver Goldsmith
painted a picture of the compassionate clergyman in 'The
Deserted Village'. The qualities remained unchanged: humility,
guidance and practical assistance:

> A man he was to all the country dear,
> And passing rich with forty pounds a year; . . .
> Unpractis'd he to fawn, or seek for power,
> By doctrines fashioned to the varying hour;
> Far other aims his heart had learned to prize,
> More skill'd to raise the wretched than to rise. . . .
> But in his duty prompt at every call,
> He watched and wept, he prayed and felt, for all. . . .
> His house was known to all the vagrant train,
> He chid their wanderings, but reliev'd their pain.

Parson Primrose, the protagonist of 'The Vicar of Wakefield'
(1766), was another of Goldsmith's characters who 'was
acquainted with every man in the parish'. Parson Primrose had a
marked effect on the lives and habits of his congregation,
'exhorting the married men to temperance and the bachelors to
matrimony; so that in a few years it was a common saying, that
there were three strange wants in Wakefield – a parson wanting
pride, young men wanting wives, and alehouses wanting
customers.'

Staunch critic of the clergy for the most part, the poet
Crabbe (who died in 1832) had a rare good word to say for the
country parson of the eighteenth century, whom at his best he
saw as an amiable and harmless friend to everyone:

> Our priest was cheerful, and in season gay;
> His frequent visits seldom fail'd to please;
> Easy himself, he sought his neighbour's ease
> Simple he was, and loved the simple truth . . .
> Mild were his doctrines, and not one discourse

But gain'd in softness what it lost in force:
Kind his opinions; he would not receive
An ill report, nor evil act believe.

The portrait was too complaisant to suggest a reflection of the poet's genuine approval. He set the parson up only to demolish him with perfect self-restraint:

Now rests our Vicar. They who knew him best
Proclaim his life t' have been entirely – rest.

Virtue and compassion revealed their more healthy aspects, blended with worldliness and common generosity, in the pages of Parson Woodforde's diary. Men like Woodforde, who was wealthier than most, recognised the responsibilities of their privileged position. They gave help where they could. There is no particular vanity in the frequency of the entries that record the parson's handouts to the poor of the parish. He also gave generously to occasional vagrants but on one occasion feared that a trick had been played on his kindness: 'To a poor Woman from Dereham by name Hall with a small Child with her was taken very ill with a violent Pain within her by my great Gates and was laid down in the road, I went out to her and gave her a good Glass of Gin and gave her sixpence to go to the Inn, but she did not go there but returned back towards Dereham. She is a Widow and belongs to the House of Industry near Dereham. I hope she is no Imposter.'

In December, 1800, the parson had another encounter with someone whom he thought was out to get the better of him: 'A Man called here this Evening about 5 o'clock had Trowsers on and had he said been a Sailor. He walked as if he was lame, he asked Charity. He appeared rather a suspicious Character & that he had other things in view than mere asking Charity, this time of the Day. I rather suspect of his being after Poultry.' Despite his doubts, the parson's natural instinct was to give the sailor money. 'As he might however be in want,' he added, 'gave him o.1.' The poultry, apparently, survived. Eleven days later,

Parson Woodforde had fifty-five poor from the parish at his house to receive their Christmas gift of sixpence each. He gave only to fifty-three of them, proving the thrifty side of his character after discovering that the other two were not members of his own parish.

The conditions that encouraged vagrants and crime became more widespread towards the end of the eighteenth century. While the parson was prospering, the poor were becoming poorer. The rising prices that provoked mild concern in Woodforde's diary caused starvation among the masses of the agricultural labourers. George Crabbe spoke out in 'The Village', in 1783, (in part an answer to Goldsmith's 'The Deserted Village'), against the 'evils of enclosure, miserable wages, insanity and often overcrowded cottages, the tyranny of some squires and many farmers'. Occasional charity was not enough.

One way of trying to help the poor out of their perpetual trap was believed to be education and in this the parson, once again, took a leading part. The Charity School movement had been started at the end of the seventeenth century by the SPCK, the Society for the Propagation of Christian Knowledge. Its aim was to provide free education by voluntary subscription but its ambitions were strictly limited by common sense. The object was to teach the children of the poor enough to enable them to read the Society's literature but not so much that they would have ideas above their station and turn against manual labour. With this philosophy, the Society hoped to allay the fears of farmers that their workforce would be depleted if they supported the scheme. The farmers were not to be persuaded. They did oppose the schools and voluntary subscriptions did not come in with the necessary speed. Although Charity Schools continued through the eighteenth century, they were not the success that had been hoped. Even in the late nineteenth century, when some farmers had been persuaded to support parish schools, the children were still taken away at harvest time, when they were needed in the fields.

The Sunday School was a less ambitious but more successful project, started up during the eighteenth century. Parsons such as Thomas Jones and John Fletcher were instrumental in getting the movement under way. The schools provided religious instruction as well as the rudiments of reading, writing and arithmetic. They rapidly became popular with the poor and acceptable to the farmers because they did not interfere with the ordinary labour of the workforce, nor with the family's regular, or not so regular, income.

The village school for the children might be run by the parson, the curate, the clerk or a specially appointed teacher. It might be sited in a room at the vicarage, in the church vestry, in a back room at the village inn or in the teacher's own cottage; there was rarely a purpose-built school-house before the nineteenth century. The teacher might be an educated woman from the village or someone brought in from outside; often the teacher would be paid for by the parson; very often the teacher might be a wholly unqualified person who was paid a mere pittance. In some cases, the parson took in pupils to live with him at the parsonage, where they were given board and lodging as well as education. This was one way in which the parson could eke out his living, by charging for the service; wealthier parsons would sometimes take in poor pupils free of charge.

Whoever taught in the school, there was never much doubt that the parson had control of it. He generally came and went as he pleased, keeping everyone in order. The rector of Berwick, Edward Boys Ellman, visited the parish school two or three times a day. If any child was absent, even for a morning, the parson went along to his home to find out what was wrong. He also held night schools at the rectory, during the winter, when the day's work was done, for those who were past school age. Parson James Lee Warner's concern for discipline in the parish school led him into a certain amount of trouble. The parson heard that a boy had been guilty of indecent behaviour and foul language in school. He pursued the boy to his home, dragged him out of the house and flogged him in the street. This was judged an intrusion of privacy and he was officially fined one shilling but he won the general approval of the community for his forthright action.

Flora Thompson remembered a typical teaching parson, in

Lark Rise to Candleford (1945): 'Every morning at ten o'clock, the Rector arrived to take the older children for Scripture. He was a parson of the old school; a commanding figure, tall and stout, with white hair, ruddy cheeks and an aristocratically beaked nose, and he was as far as possible removed by birth, education and worldly circumstances from the lambs of his flock. He spoke to them from a great height, physical, mental and spiritual. "To order myself lowly and reverently before my betters" was the clause he underlined in the Church Catechism, for had he not been divinely appointed pastor and master to those little rustics and was it not one of his chief duties to teach them to realize this? As a man, he was kindly disposed – a giver of blankets and coals at Christmas and of soup and milk puddings to the sick.'

A Schools Inspector was clearly impressed by what he discovered as he travelled round the countryside in the 1840s: 'I have looked carefully over my lists,' he wrote, 'and I can find only nine instances out of 200 where I have not reason to think that the clergyman has a deep interest in his school, not shown only by words but by watchful care and frequent attendance.' Charles Kingsley, arriving in his new parish of Eversley, also in the 1840s, discovered, in contrast, that the village school was 'a stifling room, ten feet square, where cobbling shoes, teaching and flogging the children went on together. As to religious instruction they had none.' Dissenters, jealous of the Anglican monopoly on parochial education, claimed that Kingsley's example was far from the exception. While the Anglicans strove to maintain their hold on the minds of young parishioners through the Church Schools, they were increasingly challenged towards the end of the century by Nonconformist and secular state schools. Elementary education became compulsory in 1880.

Kingsley's concern for the people of Eversley revealed itself, outside the school, in a vigorous and positive brand of practical Christian socialism. Although he was not in favour of such extremes as strikes, he did much to encourage working-men's associations and planned energetically for better sanitation and for adequate medical services in the countryside. There were others, like Kingsley, who believed in practical social help. Parson Henslow of Hitcham, a friend of Charles Darwin, let out portions of his glebe as allotments for agricultural labourers, to encourage them to supplement their meagre incomes. The local farmers objected that this would increase the expectations of the workers and would damage their own source of cheap labour. They threatened to sack any man who took an allotment. Henslow immediately let out fifty-two such allotments and the number trebled over the years. Parson Girdlestone of Halberton in North Devon went further. When the farmers objected to him preaching against low agricultural wages in the 1860s, he arranged jobs in other counties for several hundred North Devon labourers and helped them to emigrate to their new employment. With the consequent shortage of labour in the Halberton area, the farmers were compelled to put up their wages. Sydney Smith was another supporter of the agricultural worker. He organised allotments for the poor at his country parishes of Foston-le-Clay in Yorkshire and Combe Florey near Taunton. Among many other causes, he espoused those of the poacher and the chimney boy.

Henslow, Girdlestone and Smith were exceptional men. Many Anglican parsons were conservative by nature; their income came from the land and they preferred not to upset the farmers or the squire by supporting controversial causes. The Noncon-formists were, on the whole, the more ardent advocates of reform and posed the greater challenge to the traditional system. Forced by this challenge to justify his existence, the Anglican parson tried desperately to involve himself in a multitude of harmless parish activities. An article in *Blackwood's Magazine* set the scene: 'The modern country clergyman is always on the go with his penny readings, harvest home festivals, church services, lectures, entertainments. He strives earnestly and laboriously to identify himself with the amusements of his people, as well as in serious things. He is anxious to show that the Church is every-where and that his sympathy is with everybody. His life is one long effort. He is always to be seen in a long single breasted coat, and slouched billy cock hat, hurrying at a half run from one end of the village to the other, intent upon some new scheme for what is called interesting the people'.

A Berkshire farmer saw no profit in all this activity and wished that the priest would leave well alone: 'Us'll never be prosperous,' he commented sagely, 'until we have fewer o' they black parsons and more o' they black pegs.' But the best kind of country parson could still win over the wary farmer by his own knowledge of rural life. George Eliot obviously approved of Parson Gilfil, 'who smoked long pipes and preached short sermons' and knew all the breeds of cows and horses. On the other hand, Parson Fellowes, who 'once obtained a living by the persuasive charms of his conversation and the fluency with which he interpreted the opinions of an obese and stammering baronet, so as to give that elderly gentleman a very pleasing perception of his own wisdom' was said by Eliot to be a man who 'has the highest character everywhere except in his own parish, where, doubtless because his parishioners happen to be a quarrelsome people, he is always at fierce feud with a farmer or two, a colliery proprietor, a grocer who was once a churchwarden, and a tailor who formerly officiated as a clerk'. Parson Fellowes understood the virtues of Parson Gilfil no better than he appreciated the underlying merits of his congregation.

The Reverend Sabine Baring-Gould told a story of a rare man, in the mould of Parson Gilfil, who managed successfully to divide his time between the two extremes of upstairs and downstairs. This parson was invited to stay with the squire for a couple of nights. He enjoyed the comforts of the squire's good bed and wine, said farewell and left by the front door. The squire's wife was somewhat surprised to meet him accidentally in a corridor two days later. The parson explained that he had re-entered the house by the back door, at the invitation of the butler, to stay with the servants. 'Like Persephone,' he told the lady of the house, 'I spend half my time above and half in the nether world.'

If such a man did not necessarily improve the social conditions of the poor, he could, at least, like W. M. Praed's parson in 'The Vicar', published in the mid-nineteenth century, embrace them all and share their pleasure and their pain:

What'er the stranger's caste or creed,
Pundit or Papist, saint or sinner,
He found a stable for his steed,
And welcome for himself, and dinner.

Praed's vicar does not only entertain in his own home: first and foremost, he is a house-going parson, who observes his prime duty, to get out among his parishioners and make himself one with them:

And he was kind, and loved to sit
In the low hut or garnished cottage,
And praise the farmer's homely wit,
And share the widow's homelier pottage.

Here, in the nineteenth century, were the same virtues as those attributed by Chaucer to his fourteenth-century parson. R. D. Blackmore, also, described the timeless ideal of a satisfactory relationship between parson and people in his poem 'Buscombe, or the Michaelmas Goose', published in the mid-nineteenth century:

The vicar loved his parish well,
And well was he loved by it,
Religion did not him compel
To harass and defy it.

But while the way of peace he shewed
Unto the Christian guerdon,
No post was he to point the road
But a man to share the burden.

The Lake District parsons were among those who came closest to understanding the problems of the land and who could always be relied on to share the people's burdens. Parson Sewell of Troutbeck in Windermere risked the wrath of his bishop to help one parishioner. The visiting bishop came trudging through the yard to look for the parson and found a man salving sheep in a shed. 'Where is the Reverend Sewell?' asked the bishop. 'Before you, my Lord,' replied Sewell. The bishop looked at the man in surprise. 'Couldn't you be better employed?' he asked. 'What better than salving my neighbour's sheep?' countered Sewell and went on with his work. The bishop had to wait until he had finished.

Such loyalty at times earned great rewards. There is a Nonconformist story from the north about a man who was sick and in danger of dying. His family did not ask their own minister to the man's bedside but instead sent for Dr Macleod from a neighbouring village. 'What church do you attend?' asked Macleod in some surprise when he arrived in the house. 'Barry Kirk,' they said. 'Why did you not call your own minister?' asked Macleod, a little irritated. 'Na, na, we would not risk him,' replied the loyal folk. 'Do you no ken its a dangerous case of typhoid?'

Toward the end of the century, it seemed that the staunch spirit of the traditional parson was beginning to weaken. Tales of love and defiance and loyalty between priest and population grow fewer. The distance between them grows greater. Contact withers and the parson turns into himself. 'I see him trudging through muddy lanes and over long sweeps of plover-haunted pastures to visit a cottager's dying wife,' wrote Samuel Butler of Parson Theobald in *The Way of All Flesh* (1903): 'He takes her meat and wine from his own table. . . . He knows that he is doing his duty . . . but then there is not much duty for him to do. He is sadly in want of occupation. . . . He does not ride, nor shoot, nor fish, nor course, nor play cricket. . . . True, he writes his own sermons, but even his wife considers that his forte lies rather in the example of his life (which is one long act of self-devotion) than in his utterances from the pulpit.'

The fictional parson in Richard Jefferies' *Hodge and His Masters* (1880) tried hard to involve himself in the life of his community but for his pains found himself criticised as much for what he did as for what he left undone: 'Years ago, when he first came to the parish, it was with determination to improve the lot of those in his care,' wrote Jefferies. 'The edge of the great questions of the day, he declared, had reached the village, and everywhere the clergy must be up and doing.' He talked with farmers and labourers at local markets, fêtes and flower shows and annual dinners; he listened unobtrusively to their opinions and delivered his own constructively and courteously; he did everything a parson could, but failed.

There were too many parties opposed to him. 'The Church is not often denounced from the housetop,' wrote Jefferies, 'but it is certainly denounced under the roof.' It was whispered around that the parson's socialising was no more than a ploy to win the people's goodwill. Tenants of his glebe threatened to quit unless he spent money on improvements but he had no money. He could not repair the leaks in the vicarage roof. He could not afford the curate that his declining strength required. He sat in his garden, keeping up appearances, with an air of confidence in the future but with no hope of thanks from his parishioners for a lifetime of work. What place was there for him in the twentieth century, if all the parish was not his home and the people not his family?

8

THE PARSON AT HOME

Nothing can equal the profound, the immeasurable, the awful dullness of this place.

Sydney Smith

O, that it was my lot to exchange this wretched, ruinous house for a comfortable cottage and a cheerful competence.

William Jones

The humble hut of the Saxon parson was a far cry from the rectory castle of the nineteenth century but it was all a man needed who lived little better than any other villager and who did not always have a family with which to fill a home. Some Norman parsons, finding this uncomfortable and unable to afford a better house, took lodgings in the local inn or stayed at the monastery which had appropriated the benefice. Others, more ambitious and richer from the profits of pluralities, built decent parsonages, with outbuildings and stables and space for entertaining the archdeacon.

The parson was deprived of his legal wife when Pope Hildebrand enforced celibacy in the eleventh century. If he required a woman he called her 'housekeeper' instead of 'wife' and kept a low profile of social respectability. The Welsh Church openly tolerated what it nicely described as 'hearthmates'. There were some men who tried hard to resist temptation and many who failed. A Worcester parson was said to have mutilated himself to avoid being tempted by local women of ill-repute and a Swalecliffe parson was accused of standing night after night listening beneath the windows of married couples. The rule of celibacy was an open invitation to scandals which mischievous critics lost no time in exposing for their own anti-clerical ends.

Clerical marriage was still forbidden during the reign of Henry VIII, though Archbishop Cranmer thought it was safe to bring his illicit wife, Joan, over from Germany. Five years later, Henry laid down severe penalties for any clergy who broke their vows of chastity. Joan and her two children went swiftly back to Germany. Parsons' wives resurfaced when the young king Edward introduced a new bill of legalisation, but they disappeared again when Catholic Mary came to the throne. After all this to-ing and fro-ing, Elizabeth was cautious and did not officially recognise clerical marriage but she tolerated it. The queen dined one day with Archbishop Parker and his wife, Margaret. Turning to Margaret as she left, she said, 'Madam I may not call you. Mistress I am ashamed to call you, so I know not what to call you, but yet I do thank you.' The parson was not permitted a legal wife until after Elizabeth was dead.

With his marriage confirmed, he then tried to make himself more comfortable at home. His wife was an expense but she helped to improve his position. Some thought her too much of an expense or simply preferred to be single. Robert Herrick lived with his maid, Prudence Baldwin, in a humble cottage in the living of Dean Prior in Devon, where, despite some grumbling against the county and his neighbours and a period of exile in London during the Commonwealth, he apparently enjoyed the simple life:

> Lord, Thou has given me a cell
>   Wherein to dwell.
> A little House whose humble roof
>   Is weather proof;
> Under the spars of which I lie
>   Both soft and dry.

A few decades earlier, George Herbert had expressed the view that the country parson should be satisfied with food that was 'plain and common, but wholesome, consisting most of mutton, beef and veal; if he adds anything for a great day or stranger, his garden or orchard supplies it, or his barn or yard.' Herrick's fare

was almost all supplied by his own garden and was even simpler
and cheaper than Herbert suggested. He shared his meals with
Prudence, who cooked them for him:

> Here, here I live with what my Board,
> Can with the smallest cost afford.
> Though ne'er so mean the Viands be,
> They well content my Pru and me.
> Or Pea, or Bean, or Wort, or Beet,
> Whatever comes, content makes sweet.

There were many richer men than Herrick: men like the
diarists Giles Moore and Ralph Josselin, who had substantial
parsonages and who survived the ups and downs of Civil War to
grumble against rising prices and soaring taxes at the Restoration.
There were also many saintlier men than Herrick: men like
Nicholas Ferrar and William Law, who turned their homes into
religious communities, where they zealously pursued a life
devoted to prayer and study as well as to charity and hard work
in an atmosphere of Christian family love.

Another seventeenth-century parson of humble circumstance
was Charles Butler, who held the living of Wootton St Lawrence
and dwelt for forty-seven years in a small, thatched cottage.
Charles Butler is known as the father of British bee-keeping and
the joy of his home was his bees. The influence of his domestic
hobby spread to his church, where he used the subject to
illustrate points in his sermons. One day, wishing to emphasise
how they should lead their own lives, he described to his congregation how they should approach a bee-hive: 'Thou must
not come among them smelling of sweat or have a stinking breath,
caused either through the eating of leeks, onions or garlic,'
he said, 'thou must not come puffing and blowing unto them,
nor violently defend thyself when they seem to threaten thee, but
softly moving thy hand before the face, gently put them by. In a
word, thou must be chaste, cleanly, sweet, sober, quiet and
familiar. So will they love thee and know thee from all other.'

John Prince was another parson, snug in his country home,

who busied himself with a particular interest in his spare time. During the forty-two years that he spent at Berry Pomeroy, between 1681 and 1723, he compiled an anthology of verses and anecdotes about the famous families of his county. Prince's *Worthies of Devon* became an extremely popular 'Who's Who' of local society and, according to one story, its influence lasted well into the nineteenth century. More than a hundred years after its publication, a young woman stalled her suitor's offer of marriage until she had checked his ancestry in her copy of the indispensable guide to good breeding. She found his family's name in the book and she married him.

The eighteenth century saw the blossoming of the country parson's domestic life. Alexander Pope described some of the benefits to which the parson might look forward:

> Parson, these things in thy possessing
> Are better than a bishop's blessing:
> A wife that makes conserves; a steed
> That carries double when there's need;
> October store, and best Virginia,
> Tithe pig, and mortuary guinea;
> Gazettes sent gratis down and frank'd,
> For which thy patron's weekly thank'd . . .
> He that hath these may pass his life,
> Drink with the 'squire and kiss his wife.

Despite the improvement in their social standing, there were many humbler men, exemplified by the fictional Parson Trulliber, who still enjoyed the atmosphere of a domestic farmyard. Fielding described how Parson Adams found Trulliber one day, 'stript to his waistcoat, with an apron on and a pail in his hands, just come from serving his hogs; for Mr Trulliber was a parson on Sundays, but all the other six days might be more properly called a farmer. He occupied a small piece of land of his own, besides which he rented a considerable deal more. His wife milked his cows, managed his dairy, and followed the market with butter and eggs. The hogs fell chiefly to his care, which he carefully waited on at home and attended to fairs; on which

137

occasions he was liable to many jokes, his own size being with much ale rendered little inferior to the beasts he sold. His voice was loud and hoarse and his accent extremely broad. To complete the whole, he had a stateliness in his gait when he walked, not unlike that of a goose, only he stalked slower.'

Parson Adams lived in circumstances just as humble, with his income of £23 a year, 'a little encumbered with a wife and six children'. His prized domestic possessions were not pigs but books. 'He had applied many years to the most severe study,' wrote Fielding, 'and had treasured up a fund of learning rarely to be met with in a university.' As with Sterne's Parson Yorick, this learning was matched to great simplicity. Goldsmith's Parson Primrose, the vicar of Wakefield, was another whose simple honesty could lead him into trouble. Primrose was a family man above all else and defended the pride of his family to the last breath in his body, but he also objected strongly to second marriages. On losing his fortune at the beginning of the book and being about to complete the marriage of his son to the daughter of a wealthy neighbour, a marriage which would have saved him from sudden and unaccustomed poverty, he learnt that the neighbour had a second wife after the death of his first. Primrose refused to compromise his principles. He broke off the engagement. 'If I am to be a beggar,' he declared outright, 'it shall never make me a rascal, or induce me to disavow my principles.' Two hundred and fifty pages later, he has led his family through a series of misfortunes, sustained their good name and recovered his money, without one exclamation against fate.

Not all parsons were so fortunate in having the support of their wives. William Jones (1771-1821), the curate, had a wife called Theodosia, who nagged him endlessly. When things got really bad, he loved nothing better than to withdraw into his study with his books and close the door firmly against all interference. So Richard Hooker, many years before, had suffered from a shrewish wife and so Thomas Hood, the poet, many years after Jones, revenged all parsons on their nagging wives in a poem that started off on the subject of the public outcry against the wearing of surplices at St Sidwell's Church in Exeter:

> For me, I neither know nor care,
> Whether a Parson ought to wear
> A black dress or a white dress;
> Fill'd with a trouble of my own, –
> A Wife who preaches in her gown,
> And lectures in her night-dress!

Samuel Butler had other problems in mind, when he raised the question of the parson's wife and family in *The Way of All Flesh* (1903): 'I have often thought that the Church of Rome does wisely in not allowing her priests to marry,' Butler wrote. 'Certainly it is a matter of common observation in England that the sons of clergymen are frequently unsatisfactory. The explanation is very simple, but is so often lost sight of that I may perhaps be pardoned for giving it here. The clergyman is expected to be a kind of human Sunday. . . . This is why he is so often called a vicar – he being the person whose vicarious goodness is to stand for that of those entrusted to his charge. But his home is his castle as much as that of any other Englishman, and within him, as with others, unnatural tension in public is followed by exhaustion when tension is no longer necessary. His children are the most defenceless things he can reach, and it is on them in nine cases out of ten that he will relieve his mind.'

Whether or not it was for any of these reasons that Parson Woodforde did not take a wife, we do not know. There is only a hint that, once, while still quite young, he was disappointed in love and he never seems to have thought of it again. Woodforde was looked after by his niece, Nancy, who went to stay with him at Weston Longeville in 1779, three years after he moved there. She was his constant companion until his death on 1 January 1803. There was a considerable age-gap between them and, not surprisingly, they had their quarrels, usually occasioned by her bouts of boredom or his bursts of criticism. 'Since our Somersett Friends left us in June last,' he wrote on New Year's Day 1791, 'my Niece hath been almost daily making me uneasy by continually complaining of the dismal Life she leads at Weston Parsonage for want of being more out in Company and having more at home, tho' I enjoy no more than herself. It was not so in 1780.'

He was right to look back in his diary to the last day of that year: 'We sat up till after 12 o'clock,' he wrote, 'then drank a Happy New Year to all our Friends and went to bed. We were very merry indeed after Supper till 12. Nancy and Betsie Davie locked me into the great Parlour, and both fell on me and pulled my Wigg almost to pieces. – I paid them for it however.' More often, Nancy and the parson whiled away the evening with a game of cards or settled down with a book. Woodforde enjoyed Fanny Burney's *Evelina* (1778) and Smollett's *Roderick Random* (1748).

It was quite common for an unmarried parson to take in a poor girl from the parish to be his housekeeper. This also relieved the girl's family of her upkeep. Parson Kinaston of Myddle, who 'kept good hospitality and was very charitable', according to Richard Gough, picked one from the family of a poor weaver, named Parks, who had eleven children. 'At the baptizing of the tenth or eleventh,' wrote Gough, 'Mr Kinaston said (merrily) "Now one child is due to the Parson", to which Parks agreed.' This joke referred to the payment of one-tenth of all produce in tithe. Gough continued: 'Mr Kinaston choase a girle, that was about the middle age among the rest, and brought her up at his own house, and she became his servant; and when she had served several years, he gave her in marriage with thirty, some say sixty pounds' portion to one Cartwright, who lived beyond Ellesmeare, and had an Estate to balance such a portion.'

John Coleridge of Ottery St Mary in Devon had a wife to look after his eccentric nature. Luckily, his was a character that endeared him to his parishioners and made him tolerated by his wife and family, among whom was his son, the poet, Samuel Taylor Coleridge (who was born in 1772). It was said that when Parson Coleridge was provided with a number of clean shirts for a stay of several days away from home, not knowing what to do with them as they got dirty, he merely wore them one on top of the other, pulling a clean one over the dirty ones whenever he required it. Another story relates how he had trouble at a dinner party with his shirt-tails hanging out. For most of the meal, he was stuffing them back, surreptitiously, into his trousers, a little perplexed by the quantity of white material that kept trying to escape. It was only when he and his neighbour rose from the table at the end of the meal that the parson found it was her dress and not his shirt he had tucked in.

John Coleridge was something of a scholar, which impressed his congregation, even though they did not understand the Hebrew quotes that littered all his sermons. Many other parsons, married and unmarried, made good use of long winter evenings in the parsonage to produce a vast output of clerical works of learning in the eighteenth and especially in the nineteenth centuries. There was James Granger, for example, vicar of Shiplake in Oxfordshire, who gave his name to the word 'grangerise'. The vicar's *Biographical History of England*, published in 1769, contained a number of blank pages in which the readers could paste their own prints cut out of other books. Eight years earlier, Stephen Hales had died, parson of Teddington and Farringdon, Fellow of the Royal Society, expert on plant and animal physiology. His experiments on the blood pressure of a horse were said by one observer to be highly disturbing but very instructive.

Working away in nineteenth-century parsonage studies, there were men like John Mossop, ornithologist rector of Covenham St Bartholomew in Lincolnshire; the naturalist, John Henslow of Hitcham; Octavius Pickard-Cambridge, squarson of Bloxworth in Dorset and expert on spiders; John Lemprière, headmaster of the Free Grammar School at Exeter, rector of Meeth in North Devon and author of a popular Victorian Classical Dictionary; the unfortunate Thomas Teasdale, curate of Luckington in Wiltshire, who laboured for ten years on a Greek Dictionary, only to be pipped at the post by the highly successful Liddell and Scott; the eccentric Parson Conybeare of Barrington in Cambridgeshire, Greek scholar and inventor, whose bicycle, which he rode long distances at night, had a seat on the front for his wife and a gunpowder flask from which he could fire sweets at

children on the roadside. One of the best-known parson–
scholars of the century was the talented Sabine Baring-Gould, the
'black squire' of Lew Trenchard in Devon, who cared for his
family parish and his own estate for forty-three years and found
time to write, among other things, thirty novels, a collection of
English folksongs, a series of books on folklore, the *Lives of the
Saints* in sixteen volumes and a number of hymns including
'Onward Christian Soldiers' and 'Through the Night of Doubt
and Sorrow'.

Such were the benefits bestowed by leisure and domestic
security on the parson and his readers but not all his output
was quite so scholarly. Praed's 'The Vicar' completes the picture
of the amateur academic busy at his desk:

> He wrote, too, in a quiet way,
>   Small treatises, and smaller verses,
> And sage remarks on chalk and clay,
>   And hints to noble Lords – and nurses;
> True histories of last year's ghost,
>   Lines to a ringlet, or a turban,
> And trifles for the *Morning Post*,
>   And nothings for Sylvanus Urban.

An air of confidence and Arcadian satisfaction encompassed
the nineteenth-century parsonage, a warm feeling of security,
the self-assurance of an unassailable Christian family civilisation.
There were known to be parishes that had their social problems,
parishes where the gulf yawned greater every year between the
parson and his people, but it was nothing to worry those whose
parsonages were at peace:

> A sweet seclusion to forget
> The world and its disasters
> And fill the mind with mignonette,
> Clove pinks and China Asters.
>
> In pensive, or in playful mood,
> To saunter here and dally,

> With leafy calm of solitude,
> Or sunshine in the valley.

This was R. D. Blackmore's description of the vicarage at Burlescombe, or Bu'scombe, in Somerset. He went on to describe the vicar reigning benignly over the parish, sharing the burden of daily life with his parishioners and ably supported by his wife:

> The vicar's wife was much the same,
> In fairer form presented,
> A lively, yet a quiet dame,
> With home sweet home contented.
>
> In parish wants and household arts
> A lesson to this glib age,
> Well versed in pickles, jams and tarts,
> Piano, chess and cribbage.

The popular parson, with his family, enjoyed a full social life and participated willingly in all activities, within church and without. Wife, daughter and son played the organ, taught in the village school and read the lesson. There was croquet and archery and tea on the lawn and interminable guests and charities to be taken round the neighbourhood and visits to London and the sea and holidays abroad. Not that the parson openly admitted that he sought these homely comforts but, though he preached equality, he could appreciate position. The fictional Simon Magus bargained with an agent for a plum living, in Gilbert's 'Bab Ballads' (1869–73). Parson Magus pretended to demand simplicity; the agent pretended to be disappointed:

> A poor apostle's humble house
> Must not be too luxurious;
> No stately halls with oaken floor –
> It should be decent and no more.
>
> No billiard rooms – no stately trees –
> No croquet grounds or pineries.

'Ah!' sighed the agent, 'very true:
This property won't do for you.'

Even so, they struck a deal.

Blackmore added another feature to the portrait of the parson's rural dream, a Keatsian touch of mists and mellowness. He watched his father, old John Blackmore, rector of Combe Martin, ride up to Exmoor to count his sheep: 'an old man with a keen profile under a parson's shovel hat, riding a tall chestnut horse, followed by his little grandson upon a stubby, shaggy pony. In the hazy holds of lower hills, some four or five miles behind them, may be seen the ancient parsonage, where the lawn is a russett sponge of moss, and a stream tinkles under the dining-room floor, and the pious rook poised on the pulpit of his nest, reads a hoarse sermon to the chimney post below.'

Some said this paradise was simply damp and cold. Even the summer had no charms for Sydney Smith, who preferred 'bad weather, coal fires, and good society in a crowded city'. 'I have no relish for the country,' he complained, 'it is a kind of healthy grave! The real use of it is to find food for cities; but as for the residence of any man who is neither a butcher, a baker, nor a food grower in any of its branches, it is a dreadful waste of existence and abuse of life.' Worse than the country were the people in it: 'I have seen nobody but persons in orders,' grumbled Smith, 'my only varieties are vicars, rectors and curates, and every now and then (by way of a turbot) an Archdeacon. There is nobody in the country but parsons.'

Parson Johnson of Nettlewell also preferred to base his life in London, rather than the country, even though he held a country living. He spent the week in London and returned to the parsonage each weekend for Sunday service. For thirty-eight years, the house was looked after by the same couple, who, believing him to have no family, looked forward to the benefits of his will. Their hopes were dashed, when the parson died, by a lady who rode down from London and declared herself to be his wife. No one in the parish had known anything about her. Parson Ellerton was another man who liked to keep his private life to himself. He placed a sign at his rectory gate, to the effect that he had quite enough acquaintances and did not wish for any more.

Parson Froude of Devon used a different kind of put-off. Acquaintances were invited to take 'pot luck' at the rectory, where their endurance would be sharply tested. Expecting something a great deal better, they were disappointed to find the table spread with hard or mouldy cheese, sour cider and stewed, unsweetened, wild green plums. 'I'm a poor man, a very poor man,' explained the parson, who was not; 'you'll have to put up with what you can get, we've no luxuries here.' Hopes were raised, though not very high, by the occasional appearance of a roast magpie, which the parson would begin to carve into minute portions. These hopes turned to despair when suddenly the parson laid down his carvers and pushed the bird aside. 'I don't like this bird. I don't fancy 'un,' he would grumble and then, with a grin at the long faces round the table, 'Let's see whether there is something better to be had.' His servant would clear away the cheese and plums and bring in a rich venison pasty, bowls of fruit with cream, good Stilton cheese and a glowing decanter of port.

Independent, country-based men like Froude and Blackmore and Woodforde, or the fictional Trulliber and Primrose, were not much concerned with putting on a public image but lived in the way that suited them best. Often enough, it suited their parishioners as well. The extent to which the late Victorian parson was divorcing himself from his roots and therefore from his people was revealed when the Victorians found difficulty in coping with the plainer facts of rural life. Francis Kilvert was apparently a man who loved the countryside but one day his nineteenth-century sensitivity came face to face with the earthy pragmatism of his eighteenth-century forbear and the encounter was revealing. It occurred when the curate surprised the family of a neighbouring parson hard at work in their yard: 'I found the two younger ladies assisting at the castration of the lambs,' wrote Kilvert in his diary, 'catching and holding the poor little beasts and standing by whilst the operation was performed, seeming to enjoy the spectacle. . . . It was the first time I had seen clergyman's daughters helping to castrate lambs or witnessing that operation and it rather gave me a turn of disgust at first. But I made allowance for them and considered in how rough a way the poor children have been brought up, so that they thought no harm of it, and I forgave them. . . . I don't think that the elder members of the family quite expected that the young ladies would be caught by a morning caller castrating lambs, and probably they would have selected some other occupation for them had they foreseen the coming of a guest. However they carried it off uncommon well.'

Kilvert's disapproval was clearly confused by a hint of curiosity at what was going on but as for the parson and his family there seems to have been little chance that they were in the least embarrassed by the curate's visit, though he suggested that they might have been. It is good to read that the parson's daughters were enjoying themselves, for, to their minds and the minds no doubt of many of their father's parishioners, they were doing nothing unnatural, nothing beyond a necessary and traditional domestic duty.

9
PARSON'S PLEASURES

The clergy haunten tavernes out of all measure and stirren lewid men to dronkenesse, ydelnesse and cursed swerynge and chydynge and fighttynge.

John Wyclif

Keep a barrel of ale in your house; and when a man comes to you with a message, or on other business, give him some refreshment, that his ears may be more open to your religious instruction.

John Berridge

Parsons are not an alien breed and no more eccentric than anyone with leisure and a lonely job might well become. They have sought their pleasures and pastimes much as other folk have done. They have been sinners and fornicators, tipplers, hunters, gamesters and gourmets. Their follies have at times been eyed benignly by their flock, at times askance. It was never so much that their own appetites waxed or waned but that the expectations of others shifted with the wind of social opinion.

What does a man do for recreation, who lives in a plain hut, perhaps without a woman, and who has laboured like his fellows in the fields all day and performed in addition the several duties of his particular calling? The medieval parson had a simple answer: he found his way to the nearest tavern, where he did as much to save men's souls by discussing the land beneath the farmers' feet as he did by discussing God over their heads in church. He won their sympathy and often their esteem. Unfortunately, harmless pleasure could become excess and esteem could turn to ridicule. Too many irregular occurrences soon fuelled the reformer's zeal.

John Wyclif did not like what he saw in the taverns of the

fourteenth century. He blamed the chess boards and the card tables that lured idle parsons in and encouraged them to sit with their drinks until they 'han lost their witt' and 'neither have eighe ne tonge ne hood ne foot to helpe hem selfe for dronkenesse'. The problem was not a new one, for a Saxon law had been needed, long before, to warn the clergy against strong drink and to counsel them to avoid 'unbecoming occupations' such as 'ale-scop and glee-man'. The same law advised the parson to 'behave discreetly and worthily', to avoid swearing and women and thieves and hunting and hawking and dicing. 'Occupy yourself with your books as becomes your order,' the Saxon law decreed. The parson, who seldom had more than two or three, either had read them each a hundred times before or more than likely could not read at all.

The clergyman who hunted in medieval times ran a much greater risk than his fellow who drank, especially if the huntsman encroached on the land of his superiors. Thomas Fleming, rector of South Molton in Devon, pushed his luck too far when he took his dogs into the park of the Bishop of Exeter in 1328 and killed and carried off some 200 wild animals. For good measure, he also seized several bullocks, some leaden and wooden troughs, some wooden benches, some carts and various other goods. Fleming was caught, arraigned before the bishop and excommunicated, a sentence from which he freed himself by paying a fine of £100. No doubt he could afford it, from the previous profits of his obviously professional expertise.

One story that is purely folklore but concerns a warning against drink also comes from Devon. The vicar of Dawlish and his clerk were on their way to Teignmouth to collect the vicar's tithes. It was a dark and stormy night and they became lost on the way. By good luck, they came across a tavern, off the road, where the lights were burning and the people making merry. The vicar was surprised to find that he knew many of the folk but had supposed each one of them to have been long since dead. They laughed at his questions, welcomed him in and filled his glass, and he and the clerk spent an evening, well content, warm and dry, drinking and dicing. The storm abated and they left but as they looked back at the inn it vanished. Bemused by this, they rode on, over a cliff, and drowned. Two rocks mark where they fell: the Parson and the Clerk.

No one with a medieval outlook could doubt that the Devil had been at work, tempting the two to ruin. The Devil's work was still the chief concern of the reformers in the early sixteenth century, when John Colet addressed the Canterbury Convocation of 1512 and summed up the state of the clergy as he saw it. He spoke of 'heretykes' and 'men mad with marveylous folysshenes' and 'the evyle and wicked lyfe of pristes; the whiche, if we beleve Saynt Barnard, is a certeyn kynde of heresye, and chiefe of all and most perillous'. He did not mention drink but we may be fairly sure that he had it in mind. Elizabeth passed a law forbidding priests 'to haunt alehouses and taverns, or any place of unlawful gaming', but with little effect. In 1567, Parson Birkbie of Yorkshire was accused of being a fornicator and of drinking and dancing in an offensive manner in a public house; he was, apparently, dressed indecently in silk breeches, with taffeta and ruffles of gold lace and he wore a sword in church. Later, the rector of Sherington in Buckinghamshire was accused of immorality on the Queen's highway and, later still, Parson Levitt of Essex was arraigned for swearing, dicing, hawking and hunting and for being 'a very careless person': he was caught in a fight with another parson at an inn near Chelmsford.

Only one sixteenth-century alcoholic tale bears the stamp of subsequent approval. This concerned Alexander Nowell, parson of Much Hadham in Hertfordshire. Nowell was a scholar and, by all accounts, a good man; he also enjoyed fishing in the nearby stream. It was his custom, in order to refresh himself during a long day's angling, to pour some beer from his barrel at home into a bottle, which he would take with him. He put a top on the bottle to stop the liquid spilling out. Once, by mistake, he left a full bottle in the long grass by the river bank for several days. When he rediscovered it, opened it and tasted it, he found that the flavour was much better than before: by which tale, Nowell is credited with the invention of bottled beer.

Another tale did at least show that there were drinking

parsons who thought of others beside themselves. Parson Walter Robert of Tiverton in Devon lived in the fifteenth century and was much given to tippling. When he died, he left in his will threepence a week to be paid to his aged mother for the rest of her days to ensure that she was provided with 'fresh drink' whenever she required it. Such thoughtfulness was worthy of a mother's love.

The Puritans of the seventeenth century, not surprisingly, put alcohol high on their list of forbidden pleasures. Accusations of drunkenness against Royalist parsons became just one of several useful levers with which to prise the opposition out of their incumbencies during and after the Civil War. One unfortunate curate was caught in a double sin at Aldeburgh, where he was indicted for 'invading a woman's bedroom at an inn at midnight with a jug of beer to get her to drink with him'. William Underwood, parson of Harby in Lincolnshire, was accused of frequenting alehouses even on the Sabbath, in the company of cobblers and pedlars and others who wasted their money on drinking and tippling. His scandalous behaviour and conversation were strongly criticised. On one occasion, he made himself 'a skorne and derision to others in haveinge the backside of his clothes besmered over with creame by those that keepe him in company'.

Despite the simplicity of his lifestyle, the poet Herrick had a taste for wine and beer and women and no regard for Puritan threats. Mortimer Collins described the richer side of Herrick's character, that lost him his living under the Commonwealth:

> Rare old Herrick, the Cavalier Vicar
> Of pleasant Dean Prior by Totnes town,
> Rather too wont in foaming liquor
> The care of these troublous times to drown.
> Of wicked wit by no means chary,
> Of ruddy lips not at all afraid,
> If you gave him milk in the Devonshire dairy
> He'd probably kiss the dairy maid. . . .
> Lover of ruby and amber wine,
> Of joyous humour and charming girls,

Hater of cant about things divine,
Of hypocrite Cromwell, and all his churls.

By the eighteenth century, there was no objection to the parson's drinking. The liquor flowed liberally at his table. Parson Woodforde was not a man to countenance excess but he took good care to stock his cellar. One evening, before he went to Weston Longeville, he entertained a small gathering to dinner at New College, Oxford, and gave them eight bottles of Port, one bottle of Madeira, some Arrak Punch, beer and cider. He was well pleased that 'I made all my Company but Dr West quite merry'; he was even more pleased that 'I carried of my drinking exceedingly well indeed.' Once established in his rectory, he turned his hand to brewing his own beer, a sensible measure of economy that was common among the country clergy and quite acceptable. Many parsons made some profit on the side by selling home-made beer to their parishioners. Alexander Pope looked about the countryside and everywhere he saw 'the parson much bemused by beer'.

Smuggling was a highly profitable eighteenth-century activity and the parson was not beyond sharing in the opportunities. Smuggled liquor often arrived at night and often in a mysterious manner. Woodforde's stocks were depleted after Christmas celebrations in 1786, so he 'had another Tub of Gin and another of the best Coniac Brandy brought me this Evening abt 9. We heard a thump at the Front Door about that time, but did not know what it was, till I went out and found the 2 Tubs – but nobody there.' In June 1788, the parson paid out more than four pounds to his man Ben for a Tub of Coniac Brandy of four gallons by Moonshine Buck, as well as two four-gallon tubs of Geneva 'and the odd 8d for Horses Shoes removed'. This last, no doubt, was to avoid disturbance. It was well to take precautions.

William Cole of Bletchley had no difficulty, with a small group of parson friends, in getting through twelve bottles of wine at a sitting: 'more than any Company I ever entertained before', noted Cole. Parson Moreton, who became parson of Willenhall in Staffordshire in 1796, could reputedly drink three bottles of wine with his meal. He was also a keen cockfighter. Parson Golty of Framlingham had a more moderate pleasure: his Tithe Book contained a recipe for gooseberry wine; maybe the recipe was given to him by one of his tithe-payers whose own wine he had enjoyed.

Extreme cases of hard drinking included the story of the parson who was so drunk that he fell into the grave while waiting for a funeral. Another clergyman disgraced himself during the parish dinner in honour of a bishop's visit and had to be carried from the table by the bishop's servants. The worst of the eighteenth-century drinkers earned the name of Bottle Companions in a sermon preached by one virtuous parson who was trying to impress the archdeacon by his own abstinence. He devoutly abhorred the habits of the fashionable clergy and accused those 'libertines' of 'immoral conduct' and of contributing to 'female ruin and wretchedness'. The vicar in Crabbe's 'The Village' presided at the table with his wig slipped sideways on his head, the clerical bands at his neck stained with wine, his leering eye rolling mischievously as he related some ribald story to loud applause. 'This merriment of parsons is mighty offensive', wrote Dr Johnson, but his indignation was countered by two lines from William Blake (1757–1827) which suggested that the mood of a congregation was no better and no worse than the mood of the incumbent:

> Then the parson might preach and drink and sing
> And we'd be as happy as birds in the spring.

Drink was nothing to the country parson, unless it was accompanied by good food. Rarely a day went by in Parson Woodforde's life without a note in his diary about what he had had for dinner. One fine dinner to which he was invited at Weston Longeville, in January 1780, consisted of 'a Calf's Head, boiled Fowl and Tongue, a Saddle of Mutton rosted on the Side Table, and a fine Swan rosted with Currant Jelly Sauce for the first Course. The Second Course, a couple of Wild Fowl called Dun Fowls, Larks, Blamange, Tarts, etc. etc. and a good Desert of Fruit after amongst which was a Damson Cheese.' He added happily that 'I never eat a bit of Swan before, and I think it good eating with sweet sauce. The Swan was killed three weeks before it was eat and yet not the lest bad taste in it.'

Eating and drinking were not the only pleasures available to a man like Woodforde. He enjoyed a variety of card games, including quadrille, cribbage, commerce, whist and loo, on all of which he laid modest stakes. At whist and quadrille, he might win or lose anything up to four shillings in an evening but, playing with Nancy in the domestic quiet of the rectory, sixpence was usually the height of their extravagance. It was not unknown, between them, for a friendly card game to spark off quite a disagreement and produce a sulk for days.

In the daytime, Woodforde liked to go out fishing, or coursing with his greyhounds, who had names like Snip and Hector and Fly. On one occasion, he recorded that his young greyhound, Hector, 'performed incomparably', but on another occasion Fly ran away with a neighbour's undressed shoulder of mutton and 'eat it all up'. This incident had an unhappy ending. 'They made great lamentation & work about it,' wrote Woodforde. 'I had the Greyhound hanged in the Evening.' In 1796, Pitt imposed a tax on sporting dogs and Woodforde paid the tax on two hounds; he did not reveal how many dogs he had at the time, so we do not know how honest or dishonest he was being.

Travelling was another considerable pleasure for Parson Woodforde. The well-off eighteenth-century parson was no stay-at-home: his horizons were wider than we might suppose. Woodforde visited Norwich frequently, for business and for entertainment. Usually, he stayed at the King's Head. He also went to Oxford on official business, as a Fellow of his old college. Sometimes, he travelled down to Somerset, to his family home at Ansford and Castle Cary and to Bath, where he had friends. Visits to London were made, also on business but to go to plays and concerts as well; Nancy liked to gaze at city sights, including the waxworks and the zoo. Other, incidental, entertainments in the life of Parson Woodforde included the circus, processions, itinerant dwarfs who exhibited their skills, a black boar that could count and Hannah Snell, a well-known female soldier, who, for a price, would relate her remarkable adventures.

Hunting was not one of Parson Woodforde's pleasures. He left that to younger men, who had the energy that Crabbe ascribed to one such playboy parson:

> A jovial youth, who thinks his Sunday's task
> As much as God or man can fairly ask;
> The rest he gives to loves and labours light,
> To fields the morning and to feasts the night.

Perhaps Woodforde had taken note of the experience of a colleague who so exhausted himself with his activities during the week that he had no stamina left with which to perform even his most basic duties on the Sunday:

> Old Parson Beanes hunts six days of the week,
> And on the seventh, he has his notes to seek,
> Six days he holloas so much breath away
> That, on the seventh, he can nor preach nor pray.

One man who wryly criticised the deplorable habits that he saw being adopted among the country clergy during the eighteenth century was the poet William Cowper, who summed up in a deft couplet the mixed feelings of amusement and chagrin that many other critics shared:

> Oh laugh or mourn with me the rueful jest,
> A cassock'd huntsman and a fiddling priest.

Despite Cowper's sniping, and that of the Methodists, hunting became an increasingly acceptable sport for the parson to enjoy. William Jones noted in his diary towards the end of the century the number of parish priests who were 'keen sportsmen, sharp shooters, and mighty hunting Nimrods of the cloth'. He added that 'For the accommodation of the latter class of these Reverends daily advertisements appear for the sale of the next presentations of valuable livings, rendered much more valuable, as being "situated in fine sporting countries", "plenty of game", "a pack of staunch fox-hounds kept in the neighbourhood".' Blind old Edward Stokes of Blaby in the prime hunting county of Leicestershire lived to the ripe age of ninety-three and managed to continue his hunting until his last years with the help of his groom, who rode beside him and rang a hand-bell to warn the parson to jump, whenever they came to a hedge or gate.

Sometimes, the keen hunting parson was hard put to it to complete the service before taking off to join the chase:

> The village bells chime, there's a wedding at nine,
> And the parson unites the fond pair;
> Then he hears the sweet sound of the horn and the hound,
> And he knows 'tis his time to be there
> Says he, for your welfare I'll pray;
> I regret I no longer can stay.
> Now you're safely made one,
> I must quickly be gone;
> For I must go a-hunting today.
> We'll all go a-hunting today,
> All nature is smiling and gay,
> So we'll join the glad throng that goes laughing along,
> And we'll all go a-hunting today.

It was in the West Country and East Anglia that the hunting parson was most often to be found in the nineteenth century; elsewhere, he still enjoyed his sport but others less enjoyed him doing so. In 1801, the unbeneficed Reverend William Daniel published a two-volume work on *Rural Sports*, which greatly shocked many clergymen. It included information on hunting, fishing, shooting, coursing and dog-breeding. Seventy years on, Parson John King of Ashby Launde in Lincolnshire was accused by the bishop of neglecting his duties, after winning the One Thousand Guineas, the Oaks and the St Leger.

Even in the second half of the century, almost a score of Devon parsons had packs of hounds and it was quite common for fox-hunting notices to be read out from the pulpit. Parson Froude had a running battle with the bishop of Exeter over these activities. On one occasion, Bishop Phillpotts went to visit Froude to have the matter out with him. Froude's men prepared a trap for the bishop by digging a pot-hole in the muddy road and Phillpotts' coach got stuck. Undeterred, the bishop proceeded on foot, declined the offer of a drink when he reached the parsonage and challenged Froude at once. 'You keep hounds,' said the bishop. 'No,' replied Froude, 'the hounds keep me. They stock my larder.' The bishop changed his tack. 'I hear rumours of drinking and fighting in the vicarage,' he said. 'There is no fighting,' replied Froude. 'I sling the men out if they get out of hand.' Unable to make further headway, the bishop left, defeated.

On a second visit to the vicarage, Phillpotts was told by the housekeeper that the parson had typhus and was in bed. The bishop withdrew in haste. Froude watched him from the upstairs window and, as soon as he had gone, prepared to go off on a good day's hunting. It was said that he stabled his horse in the vestry, so that he could join the hunt immediately after the service. Phillpotts does seem to have been something of an innocent on the subject of hunting, from the moment that he arrived in the diocese. He watched a group of huntsmen galloping across a field and expressed surprise at the number that were dressed in mourning. Those were his parsons, he was told. His subsequent encounters with Froude did at least sharpen his wit. 'I am told, my Lord, that you object to my hunting,' said an outraged vicar. 'Dear me,' replied the bishop, perhaps in some despair, 'who could have told you so? What I object to is that you should ever do anything else.'

Froude himself was made the object of a piece of trickery by another well-known hunting figure, Jack Russell, perpetual curate of Swimbridge near Barnstaple. Russell once attempted to sell Froude a blind horse. Horse-dealing was Russell's greatest pleasure and he was reputed to have got through thousands of pounds of his wife's money on his own horses. He was also renowned for the long distances that he would ride to a meet, even in old age. One day, in 1876, when in his late seventies, he left a hunt near Ivybridge in South Devon at two o'clock and rode seventy miles across Dartmoor to reach Swimbridge at eleven o'clock in time to get some sleep and be up for another ride the next day. The year before this feat, he attended a ball at Sandringham, given by the Prince of Wales on New Year's Eve, and danced with the Princess of Wales late into the night. He died at the age of eighty-eight and his funeral at Swimbridge was attended by more than a thousand people from all walks of life.

Jack Russell had his own confrontation with authority, when Bishop Phillpotts forbade him to keep a pack of hounds. The curate blandly promised to do as the bishop wished and, for once, Phillpotts felt that he had gained a point, but Russell had a surprise for him. 'Of course I must obey you, my Lord,' he said with cunning, 'but I will tell you at once that I shall give the hounds to my wife.' Not all bishops were as intolerant of the hunt as Phillpotts. One gave his permission to a parson to hunt, provided that the man promised to accomplish all his normal duties at the same time and avoided getting into debt and, above all, that he rode straight to hounds. 'If I hear of you craving or shirking,' said the bishop sternly, 'I shall withdraw my permission at once.'

The parson's love of the chase was epitomised by the tale of the parson of Bradwell-on-Sea, who was so fired with determination to be in at the kill that he pursued the fox up on to the chancel roof. A traditional West Country song records another lover of the chase, the virile, vigorous Parson Hogg:

> And every day he goes to mass
> He first draws on the boot, Sir,
> And should the hounds perchance to pass
> He'll join in the pursuit, Sir.

Parson Hogg 'little loveth prayer' but 'dearly loves the horn'. He preached without book and to a single theme, the text of which provided his chorus:

> Sing tally-ho! sing, tally-ho!
> Sing tally-ho! Why, zounds, Sir!
> He'll mount his mare, to hunt the hare,
> Sing tally-ho! the hounds, Sir!

157

Parson Crawley, from Thackeray's *Vanity Fair*, spread his sporting activities far beyond the hunting field, though riding to hounds was not forgotten; nor was riding the social circuit. He was 'a tall, stately, jovial, shovel-hatted man, far more popular in his county than the baronet, his brother', wrote Thackeray. 'At college, he had pulled stroke-oar in the Christchurch boat, and had thrashed all the best bruisers in the "town"'. He carried his taste for boxing and athletic exercises into private life: there was not a fight within twenty miles at which he was not present, nor a race, nor a coursing match, nor a regatta, nor a ball, nor an election, nor a visitation dinner, nor indeed a good dinner in the whole county but he found means to attend it.' Needless to say, Crawley's fine voice, with which he paid for his dinner by singing 'A Southerly Wind and a Cloudy Sky' to the delight of the assembled company, could also be heard 'giving the "whoop" in chorus with general applause' in the field. 'He rode to hounds in a pepper-and-salt frock,' added Thackeray, 'and was one of the best fishermen in the county.'

The poet Crabbe included fishing among his list of a parson's mild amusements:

> Fiddling and fishing were his arts: at times
> He alter'd sermons, and he aim'd at rhymes;
> And his fair friends, not yet intent on cards,
> Oft he amused with riddles and charades.

In the nineteenth century, fishing remained very popular. There was one north-country parson who harnessed the energies of the village children to collect minnows for him every Saturday during the fishing season, for use as bait. The minnows were kept in the font over the weekend in preparation for the parson's regular outing on Monday. When a young mother unwittingly asked the sexton to arrange for her baby to be baptised on a Sunday, she was told brusquely that it was impossible: the parson's minnows could not be moved.

Sometimes parishioners protested at the sporting activities of their parson. 'There's nothing in the Bible to say that the

Apostles went out shooting game,' declared a man who did not like his parson going after rabbits. 'No,' replied the parson, 'sport was bad in Palestine. They went fishing instead.' At other times, it was the parson who objected to the sporting activities of his parishioners. Francis Kilvert noted in November 1871: '"What a fine day it is. Let us go out and kill something." The old reproach against the English. The Squire has just gone out with a shooting party.'

Some sports gained in popularity because they appeared to be relatively harmless. Archery and croquet were genteel occupations to enjoy on the vicarage lawn. Cricket benefited greatly from the enthusiasm of the country parson. In 1828, the Reverend Lord Frederick Beauclerk, a former president of the MCC, brought his talents to the parish of Redbourn in Hertfordshire. Not for him the reservations of a man like Henry Venn, another keen cricketer, who, when he became a priest in 1749, laid aside his bat with the words: 'I will never have it said of me, "Well struck, parson!"'

Alcohol, on the other hand, was no easier to lay aside in the nineteenth century then it had been in the eighteenth, and smuggling became even more of a business than it had been in Parson Woodforde's time. 'Brandy for the parson, Baccy for the clerk': that was how Kipling saw the smuggled goods dispersed. The church was always a useful place to hide the contraband. Charles Burton, for sixty years rector of Lydd in the Romney marshes, received casks of brandy that were off-loaded at Dungeness Point and brought by horse to be stored beneath the tiered seats on either side of his nave. On one memorable and nearly disastrous occasion, one of the casks split open in its hiding place and spread unmistakable fumes of liquor throughout the church just in time for Sunday service. A quick-witted churchwarden pretended to faint and was hastily revived by a colleague with quantities of brandy sufficient to obscure the original source of the smell.

Many of his parishioners no doubt benefited from and approved of Parson Burton's activities. Many an isolated rural parson who had a drink problem was often regarded with no worse than mild amusement by his tolerant congregation. On a visit to a wild Devonshire moorland parish, a stranger is said to have stopped a woman and asked her to show him where to find the vicar. 'Did 'ee see a man go by on a white horse?' the woman asked. 'I did,' replied the stranger. 'An' was he blind drunk?' asked the woman. 'He certainly was rolling in the saddle,' said the stranger. 'An' was he cursin' and swearin' fit to burn his tongue out?' the woman asked. 'He was using very shocking language,' agreed the stranger. 'Ah, then,' the woman sighed, 'that's our parson. An' a dear good man he be.'

Baring-Gould had a story of a hard-drinking, north-country parson who was challenged to identify a number of vintage wines while blindfolded. He named each one correctly, until the last, which puzzled him. 'What do you make of it?' asked his challenger, in triumph. 'Beastly stuff,' replied the parson, 'never before had my mouth full of such rubbish!' His eyes were unbandaged. The glass contained water. Parson West was another man of the cloth renowned for his intemperance and his refusal to drink water. A neighbour mentioned that he had heard the parson owned a remarkable fresh spring on his glebe. 'Oh, yes, beautiful! surpassing!' West exclaimed. 'Water so good that I never touch it. Afraid of drinking too much of it!' he laughed.

Baring-Gould also had a drinking story of an old scholar–parson, whose simple pleasures brought him closer to his congregation. When a labourer in this particular parish wished to have his child privately baptised, he would provide 'a bottle of rum, a pack of cards, a lemon, and a basin of pure water' and then he would send for the parson and the farmer for whom he worked. When the parson had performed the baptism, with the farmer as witness, the basin was taken away, the table was cleared and the cards and the rum were brought out. 'On such occasions,' wrote Baring-Gould, 'the rector did not return home till late, and the housekeeper left the library window unhasped for the master but locked the house doors. Under the library window was a violet bed, and it was commonly reported that the rector had on more than one occasion slept in that bed after a christening. Unable to heave up his big body to the sill of the window, he had fallen back among the violets, and there slept off the exertion.'

In 1892, after some difficulty, the Clergy Discipline Act was passed. Drunkenness thenceforth became an offence to be punished by the loss of a living. This did not stop drinking, nor gaming, nor hunting, but the twentieth century took its share of pleasures in moderation.

10

THE TWENTIETH-CENTURY PARSON

He was a parson, so his job in life wasn't an easy one . . .
but he slogged away at it.

Alan Miller

If he is prepared to have a breezy word for everyone . . . he
and his family will be tolerated. But if he teaches religion . . .
he will be despised and rejected when not actually mocked.

John Betjeman

The country parson has experienced a revolution in his circumstances during the twentieth century. Social and economic earthquakes have upset the old balance within the country parish (though many would say they have righted the old imbalance). The parson and his parishioners are no longer bound together inextricably by common and material interests. No longer is the church or chapel the focus of the community.

Yet the parson is still here, still trying to perform his traditional duties, and here are we still curious about his habits, good and bad. 'What a pity it is,' said Sydney Smith, 'that we have no amusements in England but vice and religion.' That may be less true today than it was in the first half of the nineteenth century, but the sentiment still has an echo. The old themes run like proven favourites through the years: the practical, theological and anecdotal. Private patronage, that ancient thorn, was still being discussed by the General Synod in 1980. Cranmer's Book of Common Prayer, first issued in the sixteenth century, still has its vigorous defenders against the challenge of the new liturgy. The parson's pleasures, his home and contacts with the people, his church and duties, money and career all demonstrate that the nature of men and their problems do not alter much, whether they live through peaceful or violent revolutions.

Alan Miller's *Close of Play* (1949) portrays a traditional country parson in the twentieth century, a man who can still blend historic ingredients into a simple life. 'Apart from his wife, whom he dearly loved,' wrote Miller, 'Septimus Jones lived for two things: his work and his cricket.' He christened the babies, tried to make the children behave themselves, married the serious lovers, appeased the quarrelsome, visited the sick and buried the dead. 'It was wearying and often disappointing labour; but to it he brought the courage, the optimism, the friendliness, and the unselfishness of an old cricketer. And remember! Cricketers are the salt of the earth!'

Cricketers and other sporting parsons survive and are still active. Between the wars, Frank Gillingham won for himself a fine reputation as a cricketing parson, playing for Essex, and since the last war David Sheppard upheld the tradition by captaining England before being ordained a deacon in 1955. The hunting parson has not vanished, either. At the memorial service for Parson Slingsby, who died when he fell off his horse while out hunting in 1912, the Archbishop of York commented, 'Hunting is a sport which develops some of the finest qualities of human courage and endurance. There are many courtesies, both to man and beast, which spring naturally from the sport of the field.' Such courtesies were not observed by opponents of the sport. In 1979, the Hunt Saboteurs Association disrupted a church service at Preston in Lancashire. The service was being taken by the rector, Canon Meredith, who was an enthusiastic follower of hounds.

The Reverend Harold Davidson, rector of Stiffkey in Norfolk, reputedly took pleasure in other things. In 1932, there was a major church scandal when the rector was accused of practising immorality with a very large number of young women. The subsequent publicity and his formal defrocking put him in the public eye and won him remarkable support. Three years later he was to be found with his daughter, each in a separate box, fasting on Blackpool beach and attracting huge crowds. They were both arrested. Davidson ended his eccentric career by preaching from inside a lion's cage in Skegness. He was savaged by the beast and subsequently died.

Food and drink remain a pleasure, for those who can afford them. The Evangelical churchman had gained a reputation long ago for being something of a glutton, perhaps because, being generally poor, he did not often have the opportunity. The Anglican, on the other hand, had a reputation for enjoying drink. The Reverend Tindall Hart recorded a story to demonstrate that this distinction was carried over into the twentieth century. A bishop, who was organising a general gathering of his clergy, was asked by the caterer whether the majority were High or Low Church. 'What difference can that make to you?' the bishop asked with curiosity. 'Well,' replied the caterer, 'if they're High Church, they drinks more and if they're Low Church, they always eats more.'

A culinary story of a different kind was told by a certain bishop who went to stay with one of his parsons for the night. The bishop came down to breakfast and was surprised to hear 'Rock of Ages' rising lustily forth from the kitchen. Pleased to imagine that this was an early morning form of worship, he asked the parson's son to tell him who was singing. 'That's cook', the boy replied. 'She always sings "Rock of Ages" when she boils the eggs for breakfast. Three verses for soft-boiled and five verses for hard-boiled.'

Life in the parsonage was not all sweet music. Large Victorian rectories, well-suited to a family of twelve, with servants and the status of a nineteenth-century parson, were blatantly anachronistic to the humble station and depleted family of his twentieth-century successor. More than that, they were impossible to run: cold, draughty, expensive and spooky. Borley Rectory in Essex was reputed to be 'the most haunted house in England', until it was burnt down in 1939. Six years earlier, a clergyman's wife had officially complained to the Church Assembly that her twenty-one-room home was too large. 'If you played a brass band in the kitchen,' she said, 'I don't think you could hear it in the drawing-room.' Another wife became so nervous that she had a dog to guard her bedroom door. It was a fierce dog and the rector was quite often compelled to shout up to her window from the garden to ask her to restrain it before he dared ascend his own staircase.

Between the wars, the parsonage still had a part to play as a centre for social welfare. There would often be a stock-pot on the kitchen range, from which bowls of soup or stew might be collected for the sick or needy. There might also be some brandy in the parson's cupboard, available for medicinal purposes on the suggestion of the village nurse, or there might be a free milk ticket at the local farm, paid by the parson, for mothers with new-born babies. Where the parson was one of the first people in the village to possess a telephone or a car, he provided an emergency service with both.

The country clergyman could still be a great many things to a great many people, even if he did no longer quite match up to the cast of characters listed by Bishop Ken, who had once held a rural living himself:

> Give me the priest these graces shall possess;
> Of an Ambassador the just address,
> A Father's tenderness, a Shepherd's care,
> A Leader's courage, which the cross can bear,
> A Ruler's arm, a Watchman's wakeful eye,
> A Pilot's skill, the helm in storms to ply,
> A Fisher's patience, and a labourer's toil,
> A Guide's dexterity to disembroil,
> A Prophet's inspiration from above,
> A Teacher's knowledge and a Saviour's love.

The parson could be none of these things if his parishioners did not allow the possibility. In the past, he had become used to criticism but his critics had generally recognised that he had a job to do. Increasingly, they did not think that he had any useful function. In 1925, Robertson Scott wrote in *England's Green and Pleasant Land*: 'In the fireside judgement of the mass of the agricultural labouring families, the average parson is witless and lazy, a self-satisfied drone, who, by the advantage of his social position, has secured a soft job, to which he hangs on, although he knows, or ought to know, that much of what he keeps on saying about the gravest matters that can engross the human mind is untrue.'

A quarter of a century later, the attitude of the average parishioner seemed to have hardened still more against the parson, according to an article by John Betjeman on 'The Persecuted Country Clergy' in *Time and Tide*, May 1951. Betjeman wrote of parsons hampered in the positive fulfilment of their duties by their rejection by those to whom their duties were addressed. He wrote of scandals spread about the parson and 'the witch-like malice of the self-righteous'; he lamented village sloth and apathy; he sighed for the man who 'sees his failure round him every day'.

Poor parson: in a changed world, the definition of his duties had not changed. It was no wonder, sometimes, that he seemed to be at sea, an alien figure shrugged off on the shoulder of a massive wave of popular unconcern. A few strong characters tried to match their message to the prevailing mood. Conrad Noel, vicar of Thaxted in Essex, was one such man. Appointed to the parish in 1910, he raised the red flag of Christian Communism and dressed in the robes of a medieval priest, much to the astonishment of his parishioners. Cambridge undergraduates took down his flag but could not extinguish his enthusiasm nor the worth of the job he tried to do, to alleviate the hardship of the people for whom he fought. Between the wars, socialist parsons preached their own vigorous message in the poorest districts, where the parson had not often been for years. Now, many parsons who might once have taken a country living find fulfilment in carrying their faith into specialist areas, to people in prisons, hospitals and factories, where they try to combine practical and spiritual help in the traditional blend. Some have been criticised for becoming unlicensed social workers.

The Church of England has also been accused of concentrating on the need to be thought 'relevant' at the expense of attention to eternal truths. Dr Edward Norman, in his Reith lectures, pointed to the sort of trendy leadership given to parish priests by, for example, the 1978 Lambeth Conference, at which he noted 'the unlikely spectacle of the bishops processing into Canterbury Cathedral to the accompaniment of The Groovers steel band – apparently intended to evoke the spirit of the Third World'. In the spring of the same year, the *Daily Telegraph* reported that a South London vicar had urged his congregation to see the film 'Last Tango in Paris' which he had described as 'a movingly acted parable'. According to that paper, the same vicar had advocated mixed saunas in Knightsbridge for which he had been warmly approved by one interested party: 'It does a lot for the image of the Church and certainly shows that not every vicar is a stodgy old fuddy-duddy.'

Back in the rural parish, the parson has had to contend with more mundane matters: the upkeep of his church and the unenviable task of raising money. His impoverishment came quickly. The inflation of two world wars hit hard. Tithes were done away with and glebe rents have disappeared or have been appropriated by the central Church body. The tradition of giving to the church declined and the wealthy could no longer be relied on to dip into their pockets to pay for major repairs or a new church bell. Popular enthusiasm for fêtes has been loyal but muted – certainly nothing to compare with the excitement of a medieval Church Ale. Appeal thermometers squeeze their thin red stems at a snail's pace up church towers desperately in need of something more substantial for support. The Church Commissioners were formed after the war, to manage the clergy's income and expenditure. In their first twenty years, money was spent on church buildings at an average of almost a million pounds a year. A large part of the burden now rests on the parishioners themselves. Strangely enough, in view of the apparent decline of church attendance, as much as one-third of the income needed to support today's parson may come from the congregation's regular contributions; the remainder is supplied by the Church Commissioners from available funds. There is, of course, always room for individual enterprise, as much today as ever in the past. In 1970, a Hertfordshire vicar appeared in a television commercial for margarine, on the understanding that he could put in a short plug for God during the advertisement. Seven years later, a

Northumbrian vicar proposed selling gravestones to visiting Americans.

Attempts have been made to revive the church itself as a meeting place for the parish, other than for services. Sometimes under pressure, sometimes eagerly, the parson has opened his doors to pop groups, choirs and concerts, to dance groups and theatrical entertainments. All kinds of children's groups meet in the church and noticeboards are festooned with parish information on clubs and outings and mutual activities. Reviving the spectre of old England, one Somerset parson brought his pet dog into church during service and successfully resisted the efforts of his parishioners to stop him by declaring that all animals were God's creatures and entitled, therefore, to enter God's house. Another image from the past was revived in 1968, when a row developed about the opening of a licensed bar in the crypt of St Mary's Church in Woolwich. The ancient right that the parishioners of Storrington in Suffolk had claimed in the seventeenth century, to have beer and cheese in church after evening service, had taken on a new lease of life.

So, too, was new life given to Parson Woodforde's refusal to baptise a child on the ground that the parents were not church-goers, when, in 1965, Parson Growns of St Augustine's Church in Guildford made a similar refusal. This subject has become increasingly disputed between parsons, who stand upon their principles or pride, and parents, who regard baptism as a basic right in a Christian country, regardless of their own beliefs. Two years earlier, a 'false' vicar was accused of dressing up in Holy Orders and of marrying a couple in Warwickshire. He was fined for the offence, which smacked of the misdemeanours of the minor clergy in the eighteenth century, who married and baptised beneath hedges at cut prices.

In and out of church, the conscientious parson might well feel overwhelmed by his duties, hurrying to and fro as fast as any nineteenth-century forebear. There are the services in church and the home-visiting and the instruction of the young for confirmation; there are the Men's Clubs and the Mother's Union and the Youth Clubs; there are Missionary Committees, liaison with the free churches, civic contacts and co-operation; there are finance and church administration and the parish magazine; there is work within the diocese and work within the parish and work within the home and time to make for private study. 'To cheer the sick and warn the sinner, to be all things to all men, and yet preserve his own self-respect and independence.' That was how Canon Thompson Elliott summed up the parson's work in *Putting Our House in Order* (1941).

It does not sound like the sort of evangelising campaign for which a young enthusiast might wish to join the church. The work of the country parson can seem mundane, poorly paid, unwelcome. Not surprisingly, most of this century has been characterised by a severe shortage of ordination candidates. At first, this was partly because of the traditional insecurity of the average curate, who could still be dismissed at the whim of his parson, but between the wars the position of the curate strengthened as scarcity of numbers forced higher demand and better terms of employment. Even so, the situation immediately after the war was bleak. In 1954, the Church Assembly complained of the shortage and encouraged the young to look at the very real contribution that the job could make to society. Numbers built up but again declined. Renewed efforts to attract candidates were made in the early 1970s but were not markedly successful. The Archbishop of Canterbury emphasised the severity of the manpower shortage in the Church.

In consequence, the Church has opened its doors wide to embrace many more possible candidates. Sydney Smith once cited the French as saying that 'there are three sexes – men, women and clergymen.' The Church is at last admitting women and has, by the breadth of its intake, done much to obscure the sharp distinctions made by Smith. There was a noticeable rise during the 1960s in the number of older men entering the Church after half a lifetime of ordinary secular employment. In 1973, six years after Parliament had passed the bill permitting homosexual acts in private between consenting adults, Dr Coggan admitted publicly that there were many homosexuals among the Anglican clergy, a statement that would have been met with shock and anger not long before and even now is disturbing to many well-intentioned people. In 1976, Conrad Noel's old parish of Thaxted shook with the news that its latest parson had been elected president of the newly formed Gay Christian Movement and had subsequently received public support from his bishop.

There has also been a widening of the parish structure, in which several neighbouring parishes have been organised so that they overlap as a single unit, cared for by a team of vicars and curates and headed usually by a rector. This change is partly aimed at resolving the simple mathematical problem of having too few parsons for too many parishes, a situation which no longer carries with it the dramatic advantage of pluralist profits; at the same time, the change provides incentives for younger men, giving them greater responsibilities within the team than they would have merely as the parson's underling. There remain many parishes looked after by one man only, though that man rarely has only one parish under his care.

Many parishioners do not like the new system and loudly proclaim the independence of their parish and its entitlement to its own parson but in too many cases their attendance figures and the available funds do not justify their complaint. Yet these people are right to care, just as they care about old and new forms of service, about Authorised and modern translations of the Bible, or about the latest attempts to update the language of traditional hymns.

Others wonder what the fuss is all about and are genuinely puzzled at what part the parson has to play in the modern community. These people are not merely cynics, nor are they necessarily apathetic. They have an important point. Their point is based on the very reasons that have brought about the decay of the villages themselves in recent decades. As so often in the past, the parson's fortunes rise and fall with those of his parish. The villages have been broken down by changes in social and economic conditions, by a revolution in transport and by increasing centralisation. The parson has almost lost his community; he has almost lost his job. The welfare state has replaced him by a battery of professional services: social workers, community leaders, counsellors, doctors, psychologists and psychiatrists, to name a few. The parson could never provide all the answers that these specialists can offer but he knew his parishioners well enough to give simple and often sound advice on a great many everyday matters. How many turn to him now, even on a problem with the very marriage that he himself celebrated? Couples are more likely to go to the doctor for a sedative or to a counsellor whom they have never met before.

There is, however, a new trend in rural life. Different economic conditions, decentralisation, the breakdown of public transport are forcing many villages to look to their own survival. The parson is needed, once again, as one of their traditional resources, not necessarily for the social or welfare services that he once used to render but for one original duty, to be the spiritual guide and companion of the people in his care. No other support group, however well-intentioned and good in practice, is trained for that task.

This need might reasonably be illustrated by a simple 'parish magazine' story told by the anonymous 'Pilgrim' who wrote a small book in 1954 describing life *In a Country Parson's Shoes*. The point of the story was that the parson could usefully have given up all his parish activities—in the local school, as an organiser of this and that, carrying out his regular services—if he could only have talked to some of the people about the spirit of life. As one little girl put it, 'I wish he had time to talk to us about religion.' She did not mean the facts of a particular faith, not semantics nor stories; she wanted him to help her understand what life was all about.

Emerson once wrote that he pitied the Church because 'she has nothing left but possession'. It was a similar complaint. What the philosopher and the country girl both wanted was something perhaps understood by the cricketing parson, Septimus Jones, the 'salt of the earth'. They wanted someone who could bring some lasting flavour to existence.

GLOSSARY

Advowson
The right of a patron to present a benefice or church office to the man of his choice, a right which itself was treated as a property to be bought and sold.

Archdeacon
Immediately below a bishop in rank, appointed by the bishop to set up courts to look into the behaviour of the laity and to conduct 'visitations' around the diocese in the intervals between the bishop's own visitations, with particular responsibility to check on the state of repair of the churches.

Benefice
A church living or estate, including buildings, land and income, given by the holder of the advowson of the benefice.

Bishop
The ecclesiastical head of a diocese or ecclesiastical district.

Chantry
An endowment for the maintenance of a priest to sing masses for the soul of his patron; usually the patron also endowed a chantry chapel, which was in the care of the chantry priest or chaplain.

Chaplain
A clergyman originally responsible for looking after a chapel and for conducting services in a chantry or private household.

Churching
Public thanks given in church for a woman after childbirth; also intended as a spiritual cleansing.

Churchwarden
Usually two churchwardens were chosen each year, supposedly by joint decision of the priest and the parish but often one was chosen by each party; originally they acted as lay representatives of the parish in church matters but they also reported to the bishop or archdeacon on the behaviour of the parson and the parishioners.

Clergy
Ordained ministers of the Christian church, including rectors, vicars and curates.

Clerk
A layman, who performed some of the minor offices of the church, leading the responses, assisting the parson in the service.

Curate
An ordained clergyman, acting as an assistant to a rector or vicar, without a benefice of his own, usually as a step towards gaining his own living. A stipendiary curate was subject to dismissal at short notice. A perpetual curate acted to all intents as the parson of a parish, under licence from the rector or patron, but by the Pluralities Act of 1838 became the official incumbent and was generally referred to as the vicar.

Deacon
The third of the major orders of the church, ranking below bishop and priest, appointed in a probationary role to assist the priest in reading the gospel and administering the chalice as well as attending to the secular affairs of the church, such as visiting the sick.

Dean, Rural
Ranked below an archdeacon, with supervisory responsibility for a group of parishes within a diocese.

Diocese
A district under the ecclesiastical rule of a bishop.

First Fruits
The first year's whole profits of a see or benefice, payable to the Pope then (after the Reformation) to the Crown, until Queen Anne's Bounty used them to raise the incomes of smaller benefices.

Glebe
Originally a clod or piece of earth; an area of land for the support of the parson within his benefice.

Incumbent
The person who holds an ecclesiastical benefice or office.

Intruder
The person who usurps the estate or rights or privileges of someone else; in this context, generally, a priest who usurps the benefice of an incumbent.

Living
A benefice, including the buildings and income belonging to a parson.

Parson
Originally a rector, the holder of a benefice, but includes vicars as well as curates. The term is often loosely applied to all clergymen.

Pluralist
A person who holds more than one living or office at the same time.

Prebend
Revenue granted to a canon or other official of a cathedral; hence 'prebendary', the holder of a prebend.

Prelate
High ecclesiastical dignitary, especially bishop and archbishop.

Rector
The holder of a benefice, with the right to all revenues of that benefice.

Sexton
Originally appointed and paid by the parish and the incumbent jointly; often also performs the office of parish clerk; responsible for keeping the fabric and contents of the church in order and for ringing the bells and digging the graves; duties generally as those of modern verger.

Sidesman
Deputy churchwarden, or assistant to the churchwarden.

Stipend
A salary or fixed payment, usually with reference to a vicar's income or to a stipendiary curate.

Tenths
The tenth part of the annual profit of every living, payable to the Pope then (after the Reformation) to the Crown, until Queen Anne's Bounty used them to raise the incomes of smaller benefices.

Tithe
Originally, a tenth part of the annual produce of the land within the parish, payable to the parson; it became commuted to a rentcharge which was eventually abolished by the Tithe Act of 1936.

Verger
The lay person in charge of looking after the immediate needs of the congregation and of taking care of the interior of the church; included many of the duties of the original sexton.

Vicar
Priest appointed by the rector as his substitute in a parish.

BIBLIOGRAPHY

Abbey, C. J. and Overton, J. H. *The English Church in the Eighteenth Century* (Longmans, 1878)

Addison, W. *The English Country Parson* (Dent, 1947)

Baring-Gould, Rev S. *Vicar of Morwenstow* (Methuen, 1903)

Barrow, A. *The Flesh is Weak* (Hamish Hamilton, 1980)

Bax, B. A. *The English Parsonage* (Murray, 1964)

Blench, J. W. *Preaching in England in the Late Fifteenth and Sixteenth Centuries* (OUP, 1964)

Brown, C. F. K. *A History of the English Clergy, 1800-1900* (Faith Press, 1953)

Carpenter, S. C. *The Church in England, 597-1688* (Murray, 1954)

Christie, O. F. *The Diary of the Rev. William Jones, 1771-1821* (London, 1929)

Christmas, F. E. *The Parson in English Literature* (Hodder & Stoughton, 1950)

Combe, W. 'The Tours of Dr Syntax', *Poetical Magazine* (1809; 2nd & 3rd Tours, 1820, 1821)

Coombs, H. and Bax, A. N. *Journal of a Somerset Rector* (Murray, 1930)

Cresswell, B. *A Book of Devonshire Parsons* (Heath Cranton, 1932)

Cutts, E. L. *Parish Priests and their People in the Middle Ages in England* (SPCK, 1898)

Daubeney, A. G. *Reminiscences of a Country Parson* (The Griffen Press, 1950)

Davies, E. W. L. *The Outdoor Life of the Rev John Russell* (Bentley, 1883)

Davies, G. C. B. *Henry Phillpotts, Bishop of Exeter* (SPCK, 1954)

Ditchfield, P. H. *The Parish Clerk* (Methuen, 1907)

—— *The Old-Time Parson* (Methuen, 1908)

Eachard, Dr *Grounds and Occasions of the Contempt of the Clergy* (11th edition, 1705)

Forbes, G. M. *George Herbert's Country Parson* (Faith Press, 1949)

Gasquet, Abbot *Parish Life in Medieval England* (Methuen, 1906)

Godfrey, J. *The Church in Anglo-Saxon England* (CUP, 1962)

Gough, R. (ed Hey, D.) *The History of Myddle* (Penguin, 1981)

Heath, P. *English Parish Clergy on the Eve of the Reformation* (Routledge & Kegan Paul, 1969)

Herbert, G. *A Priest to the Temple; or the Country Parson, his Character and Rule of Holy Life* (2nd edition, London, 1671)

Hoskins, W. G. *The Leicestershire Country Parson in the Sixteenth Century* (Thornley, 1940)

Jarvis, K. *Diary of a Parson's Wife* (Mowbray, 1958)

Jefferies, R. *Field and Hedgerow* (London, 1888)

Josselin, Rev R. (ed Hockliffe, E.) *Diary*, Camden 3rd Series, vol 15 (Camden Society, 1908)

Kilvert, Rev R. F. (ed Plomer, W.) *Diary*, 1870-79 (3 vols, Cape, 1938-40)

McClatchey, D. *Oxfordshire Clergy*, 1777-1869 (OUP, 1960)

Moorman, J. R. H. *A History of the Church in England* (Black, 1953)

Owst, G. R. *Preaching in Medieval England* (CUP, 1926)

Pearson, H *The Smith of Smiths* (Hamish Hamilton, 1934)

Pilgrim *In a Country Parson's Shoes* (Skeffington, 1954)

Purvis, J. S. *An Introduction to Ecclesiastical Records* (St. Anthony's Press, 1953)

Rous, J. (ed Green, M. A. E.) *Diary*, 1625-42 (Camden Society, 1856)

Savidge, A. *The Foundations and Early Years of Queen Anne's Bounty* (SPCK, 1955)

Smyth, C. *Church and Parish* (SPCK, 1955)

Stackhouse, T. *The Miseries and Great Hardships of the Inferior Clergy in and around London* (London, 1722)

Stokes, F. G. *Bletcheley Diary of the Rev. William Cole* (Constable, 1931)

Tindall Hart, A. *Clergy and Society*, 1600-1800 (SPCK, 1968)

—— *Country Counting House* (Phoenix House, 1962)

—— *The Country Priest in English History* (Phoenix House, 1959)

—— *The Curate's Lot* (John Baker, 1970)

Tindall Hart, A. and Carpenter, E. *The Nineteenth Century Country Parson, c. 1832-1900* (Wilding, 1954)

Trotter, E. *Seventeenth Century Life in the Country Parish* (CUP, 1919)

Walker, J. *Sufferings of the Clergy* (London, 1714)

Watt, M. H. *The History of the Parson's Wife* (Faber, 1943)

West, F. *The Country Parish Today and Tomorrow* (SPCK, 1960)

Whitaker, W. B. *Sunday in Tudor and Stuart Times* (Houghton, 1933)

Woodforde, Rev J. (ed Beresford, J.) *The Diary of a Country Parson*, 1758-1802 (5 vols, OUP, 1924-31)

ACKNOWLEDGEMENTS

I would like to thank Sarah Wallace for her encouragement from the start and for her editorial supervision and perseverence which ensured that the book was published; Peter James, for the care with which he criticised and corrected the typescript; Anne-Marie Ehrlich, for undertaking the picture research.

INDEX

INDEX

Toplady, Augustus, 108
Trollope, Anthony, 55, 88, 95
Troutbeck, 131
Trulliber, Parson, 137, 145
Trusler, John, 94–5
Turner, Dr, 25
Turner, Michael, 109
Twenty-four Articles, The, 20
Tyburn, 28
Tyndale, William, 16

Udal, John, 20
Underhill, Thomas, 17
Underwood, William, 150

Venables, Parson, 56, 58, 84
Venn, Henry, 159
Vesey, Bishop, 64
Vicar of Bray, The, 28–9
Vicar of Wakefield, The, 30, 124, 138

Walker, Rev J., 23
Warham, 109
Warner, James Lee, 127
Warwickshire, 74
Waterbeach, 35
Waterloo, Battle of, 36
Water Stratford, 92
Webster, Thomas, 52
Welshe, Robert, 18
Wesley, Charles, 32, 108

Wesley, John, 32, 35, 108
Westmorland, Earl of, 20
Weston Longeville, 69, 139, 151, 152
West, Parson, 160
White, George, 35
Whitfield, George, 32
Whitgift, Archbishop, 20, 58
Whitney, Hannah, 98–9
Wilberforce, Samuel, 36
Willenhall, 151
William of Orange, 28
William of Wykeham, 16
Williams, Eleanor, 84
Williams, Parson, 98
Wilton, Thomas, 17
Wiltshire, 141
Windermere, 131
Wiveliscombe, 86
Woodforde, Parson, 30, 67, 69–70, 82, 83, 95, 125, 126, 139–40, 145, 151, 152–4, 159, 168
Woodley, 72–3
Woodmancote, 115
Woolwich, 168
Wootton St Lawrence, 136
Worcester, 134
Wyclif, John, 16, 63, 147

Yorick, Parson, 94, 138
York, Archbishop of, 18–19, 102, 163
Yorkshire, 48, 57, 129, 149